Praise for *Writing Without a Parachute*:

"Here is a book that charts new territory, inviting the
writer to fall with confidence into the ether of the creative
self in order to write with skill and authenticity."
Louise Green, Editor, Lapidus Journal

"One of the sanest books on writing I've ever read."
Susan Lynn Reynolds, Byline Magazine

"Useful for beginners, superb for writers in the middle of their training
and an absolute lifesaver for pros who have lost their nerve."
Mimi Thebo, Department of Creative Writing, Bath Spa University

"Read this book…"
Richard Moss, M.D., author of The Mandala of Being *(New
World Library) and* The Black Butterfly *(Celestial Arts)*

by the same author

Writing Without a Parachute
The Art of Freefall
Barbara Turner-Vesselago
ISBN 978 1 78592 171 1
eISBN 978 1 78450 443 4

Freefall into Fiction
Finding Form

Barbara Turner-Vesselago

I would love to know if this is helpful, Hedda. We will talk of ins & many Thys... with my best wishes,

Barbara

Jessica Kingsley *Publishers*
London and Philadelphia

First published in 2017
by Jessica Kingsley Publishers
73 Collier Street
London N1 9BE, UK
and
400 Market Street, Suite 400
Philadelphia, PA 19106, USA

www.jkp.com

Library of Congress Cataloging in Publication Data
Names: Turner-Vesselago, Barbara, author.
Title: Freefall into fiction / Barbara Turner-Vesselago.
Description: London ; Philadelphia : Jessica Kingsley Publishers, 2017. |
Includes bibliographical references and index.
Identifiers: LCCN 2016027507 | ISBN 9781785921728 (alk. paper)
Subjects: LCSH: Fiction--Authorship. | Fiction--Technique. | Creative writing.
Classification: LCC PN3355 .T87 2017 | DDC 808.3--dc23

British Library Cataloguing in Publication Data
A CIP catalogue record for this book is available from the British Library

ISBN 978 1 78592 172 8
eISBN 978 1 78450 442 7

Printed and bound in Great Britain

Acknowledgements

Several people have profoundly shaped my understanding of meaning and how it finds expression: Professor George Whalley, Julia Press, and Dr. Richard Moss, in particular. The late Professor Whalley's teaching and his book, *The Poetic Process*, have been a major influence, as have Richard Moss's unflagging efforts to find new ways to speak about the infinite. Julia Press, simply by the way she lives her life, has given me an intimate awareness of what it means to embody grace. I cannot imagine her wanting to go anywhere she could not hold the door open for whoever wants to follow. I have also been blessed to have had some excellent writers as mentors: W.O. Mitchell, Timothy Findley, and Jack Hodgins.

A gifted editor is the greatest boon a writer could wish for, and Sarah Bird is one of those. So much that is here has benefitted from her insight, patience and steadiness, as well as from her wisdom as to how to best convey them. Sarah, it has been a privilege from the outset to work with you, and I am so grateful.

I would also like to thank Michaela Meadow, once again, for the lovely cover design and for being so easy to work with. Thanks, too, to Denis Kennedy, for his assiduous copy editing, and for knowing where to draw a line between informality and sloppiness, and to Alan Blakemore and Wayne Sercombe, for so happily giving their time to proof reading.

My gratitude goes to everyone involved with the Vala Publishing Co-Operative, for the faith, vision and hard work that has helped to bring so many wonderful books into being, and especially Sarah Bird, whose vision birthed Vala in the first place.

Vicki Pinkerton, thank you for working on permissions, and for picking up so much slack in your role as the Freefall Writing Assistant.

Clare Bolton, thank you for your earlier work on permissions, which made that part of the book so much easier to do.

I don't think I could have written this book if I weren't actively involved in the present with people's writing. I am very grateful to all the people who currently make this possible by organising the workshops: Devon Ronner, Kirsten Cameron, Jane James, Rosemary Stevens, Mel Jones, and Nicki de Hoog. And I continue to thank all those who worked so hard in this way in the past: Marigold and Richard Farmer, who brought my work to England, the late Margaret Curl, who did the same in Australia, Kim Roberts, Kaye Gersch, Nicola-Jane LeBreton, Geoff Mead, Frances Horibe, Yvonne Hunter, Lelle Taffyn, Gill Goater, Bob Thornhill and so many others over the years.

Financial contributions and companionship during the writing process were provided by the ninety-plus people who joined the crowd-funding campaign on Indiegogo, all of whose support was to me invaluable. In particular, I would like to mention Tom Ohaus ("Platinum Supporter"); Nancy Thomson ("Gold Supporter"); and Elizabeth Beatty, Bernadette Brady, Manning Guffey, Craig and Val Johnstone, Marie Lauzier, Wendy Murray, Susan Pogue, Sharad Sharma, and Deepam Wadds ("Silver Supporters").

As always, my husband, Michael Vesselago, has supported me in every way possible during the writing of this book, even at the very latest stages when I inevitably met his suggestions for the stuck places with skepticism ("How could you possibly understand this problem?") soon to be replaced by relief ("That's really insightful") and the sense that I could move on again, burden shared. Michael, I don't know how you do it, but I know it starts with empathy, the great gift you give to the world so freely.

To Michael Vesselago: You. Everywhere. Now. Always.

Contents

Preface

In *Writing Without a Parachute: The Art of Freefall,* I emphasise the
fact that writing is not the same as thinking. Writing will always
be a voyage of discovery: it takes you to new places and new
understandings you would never have anticipated merely by thinking.
At this juncture in your writing life, when you've become experienced
in the practice of Freefall Writing and would like to take your work
further, this point may be better expressed as, "Writing is not the same
thing as thinking about writing". Writing will almost always provide
you with insights more unexpected and germane to your writing than
merely thinking about it ever can. Yet we are creatures who can think
and learn in other ways – yes, even about writing – and apply that
learning in our own writing even while we are deeply under its spell.
In fact, doing so seems to constitute an important element of seeing a
more intentional project – a short story, a novel, a memoir, or a poem –
through to the stage where it can be shared with other people. Even if
we choose not to use what we know, knowing gives us a choice.

It has always been my intention to write two companion volumes
about Freefall Writing, the first of which would help writers to experience
all that Freefall Writing has to offer, while the second would explore
the subsequent process of using Freefall in a more intentional way
within a genre (such as fiction, memoir, or poetry). This book, *Freefall
Into Fiction: Finding Form,* is the fulfilment of that second purpose, and
reflects my best understanding thus far of how, as writers, we can bring
what we know to the service of our writing.

Since, like me, most of the people I work with are primarily interested
in writing fiction and memoir, you will find that much of what I say
here is directed towards work in those two genres. But because much
of the "making" (*poesis*) that goes into these forms of writing is the

same across all the genres, including poetry, I believe that, even if your main interest lies in making poetry, you will find much that is directly applicable to that undertaking here.

Like *Writing Without a Parachute*, this book is structured so that you can use it either as a reference or as a writing course, to be undertaken alone or with your writing partner/s. I strongly recommend that, in either case, you do at least some of the "Writing Experience" suggestions as you go along, even if they feel foreign to you. I say that not because I think you need more duties to perform, but because the practice of writing leads to a greater understanding of what I'm talking about in each chapter than thinking ever can. Bringing some intention into your work in this way, a little at a time, will not threaten the hard-won freedom you have nurtured thus far.

It's important to treat writing as a relationship: to be curious, yes, and to try out new things, but at the same time to *stay aware of what helps the writing to flourish and what does not*. And that is what I would ask you to do as you read this book. Although I have tried to write it from a writer's point of view, it's actually very difficult to talk about writing without standing back from that experience. So when I make any sort of generalisation about writing, my hope is that you will continue to observe your own response, and honour your own relationship with writing, rather than try to force yourself to be objective about it. There are times when you need some objectivity, in order to make a bridge for yourself into something new, and times when you need to engage with the writing in order to do that, no matter what stage you've reached in the process.

I recently heard one workshop participant, an experienced writer who now has four published novels to her credit, announce on the third day, "If I say to myself I'm writing a novel, it doesn't help me one bit. I just have to get in there and look around". And that's just about saying to herself that she's writing a novel.

Writing, even within a genre, will always call for both will and surrender in varying measures. Now and throughout your writing life, you will have to find – and keep on finding – your own unique balance between the two.

Chapter One

Taking it Forward

I n my view, the only truly beneficial approach to writing is one that helps the writer move beyond the dictates of the practical, egoic self, to touch into the vaster creative potential that we all have, but normally don't connect with, although we may catch a glimpse of it in meditation, or marvel at it in our dreams. Once we have found a reliable way to gain access to that more unfettered realm of possibility, we become empowered to create something truly new and authentic – the product of our own unique and resonant writing voice.

The first step, then, is to learn to connect with this wider field, and experience what becomes possible in writing when the intending ego can be set aside. This is the stage of writing with an open heart, able to let things emerge on the page that you haven't anticipated; it is the stage in which you become skilled at surrender. It was the purpose of *Writing Without a Parachute: The Art of Freefall* to provide a reliable guide for this kind of exploration and a systematic approach to its deepening.

Once a writer has established a fundamental trust in the experience of writing as one of freedom, curiosity and discovery, the next step involves bringing some measure of intention back into the process. This is the stage in which the writing finds its form, as all writing must to some extent find form, within the traditions of a recognisable genre (such as fiction, poetry, or memoir). But it is crucial that this step be taken *without* sacrificing the ability to surrender. Finding (and re-finding) an appropriate balance between those two impulses, intention and surrender, is what the act of writing now entails.

In *Writing Without a Parachute*, I described the ecstatic days at Cambridge that led me to search out the fundamental principles of Freefall Writing. That search was greatly assisted, as I observed there, by my experiences with my writing students in Nigeria, and in W.O. Mitchell's studio at the Banff School of Fine Arts, both of which strengthened my grasp of the terms of that surrender. But as valuable as they were, neither of these experiences had much to offer with regard to undertaking this second stage of writing. Yes, some of my Nigerian students published the novels they had written so freely, but those were celebrated largely as "naïve" novels – valued as much for their energy and raw intuitiveness as for the little-known cultures they conveyed. At Banff, W.O. would tell me with his sly chuckle, "Just slap an ending on this piece of writing. Oh, it'll feel so wrong to you. It'll feel so phoney. But they'll never notice the difference!" Thrilled though I felt to be given what seemed like inside information from a writer I so admired, he was right – it didn't feel good. It felt arbitrary and artificial just to "slap" an ending on a spontaneous piece of writing. It worked a few times, in that the piece was published, but I didn't come away with any further understanding of how powerful works of fiction – or memoir – are made.

For that, I have had to draw upon a lifetime of experience in writing and the study of writing, and on that of my students in the hundreds of writing workshops I have given since then. I've come to see that while unknowing plays a vital part, knowing is important, too. Energy (and often fear) plays a role, but so does experience. In each moment of writing, there's the balancing and re-balancing of hope and intention with whatever is being discovered in that moment, so that the new can unfold within the confines of a known (or at least recognisable) situation.

~

I can now see, looking back, how the seeds for a fundamental understanding of all of this were sown during and soon after that awakening experience at Cambridge. But I could never have appreciated that at the time. Perhaps that's because, as central to the rest of my life as what I was learning was to become, the degree of unknowing – of fear and often real terror – bound up with that learning was so profound.

For part of my time as a doctoral student at Cambridge, I lived in the flat of a manor house on the Isle of Ely, a promontory that lies to the east of Cambridge, surrounded by farmland reclaimed from the fens. Month after month, I tramped those black fields in bitter winds said to blow straight from the Ural Mountains, with a feeling of despair, unable to write my thesis and beset by convictions of my own unworthiness to do so. How could I presume to know something no-one had said before? What could I ever say that would be truly new? And yet that was what I had to discover in my doctoral research: something new! My whole future – not to mention my current livelihood (a substantial doctoral fellowship) – depended on it.

My despair only worsened with the onset of Bell's Palsy, a potentially disfiguring virus that, along with all my windswept walks, gave new meaning to the old saw, "If the wind changes, your face will stay that way." I began to discover that the state of fear I was living in had slipped beyond my conscious control: the very "I" that had so obsessed me of late had become increasingly difficult to locate. Now, as I walked, the ground seemed to pass under me as if it were a film, with no sense of myself as an experiencing ego in the midst of it. This didn't change when I walked in our kitchen door, or lay awake in bed at night. My dreams, when I did sleep, were astonishing, technicolour productions filled with departing regiments, and firemen who struggled to subdue spewing volcanoes. I was convinced I was going crazy, and terrified about what the rest of my life might look like.

Then one morning, after a long night of terror, as I stood in the kitchen watching the sun come up, that fathomless fear and unknowing began to shift into something very different. From between my ribs, there seemed to pour a blissful stream of energy of which all things, and I too, I now realised, were a part. It seemed to radiate from the rising sun into the centre of my being and back out again, even as I was being dissolved into all that was. The boundary between subject and object had vanished. Whatever the ultimate source of this energy that constituted the world might be, I knew that it was good.

Perhaps the very thing that I had found so terrifying, the loss of self, had made it easier to perceive this. There was simply nothing left of me to get in the way. Without even knowing such a thing could happen, I had been plunged into what felt like a deeper level of reality that underlay all I had known and assumed about the world – and from which I was inseparable. I was it, and it was me. It was enough simply to rest into that unending stream of becoming.

As the days went by, I realised that I had no idea how to take this forward. How could I continue to live this experience in the midst of the practical demands of daily life – like buying food, paying rent, and writing a Ph.D. thesis? Yes, I had heard the story of a woman in India who lay on the grass for two years in some kind of rapture, sustained by a cow that came along and fed her from its udder. But this seemed unlikely to happen on the Isle of Ely. All I wanted was to spend a year or two examining everything I had previously thought I knew in the light of this new awareness. But how could I remain in this ego-less state, and yet read, write, and thereby earn money, at the same time? How could I, in other words, impose my will on the situation – long enough to keep receiving my fellowship – without sabotaging this rapturous state of surrender?

As weeks passed, and the realities of my situation began to press in on me, I began to tell myself, "You need to shut this down a bit. You've got to find a way to put it on the back burner so you can get some work done."

However, as I started to pull the fragments of my personality back together, I found it wasn't so easy to keep that back burner going. For several weeks, I walked around Tesco and the University Library with what felt like a lightbulb glowing between my ribs, reassuring me that it was still possible to stay in touch with that deeper level of being as I forged through the welter of my days. But the better I got at forging through them, the dimmer my inner lightbulb seemed to grow. Before very long, I realised with enormous sadness that I was referring to a memory, rather than living my newfound awareness as a direct experience. The immediate experience of awakening was over, at least for now, though it had changed my orientation to life radically and forever.

One of many things it had left me with was the ability to recognise, often instantly, what pertained to that deeper knowing when I came across it. I seemed to have become a sort of human Geiger-counter. Because this held true for writing, it allowed me to come to a new understanding of the inner workings of creativity, which in turn led to the evolution of the precepts of Freefall Writing. But that was only one aspect of this knowing. Whenever something I encountered, either within myself or outside of me, didn't manifest that deeper current, I could feel it. If it did, and especially if it made the current grow stronger, I knew that too.

I was also very well aware that if I had had this experience, and now knew this much about the nature of reality, there must be people out there who knew immeasurably more. But how was I to find them? I would still talk about my experience with anyone who would listen – a bit feverishly, in fact. If I even got near the subject, I didn't seem to be able to stop talking about it. But most of my friends at Cambridge had just shaken their heads. A year or two later, when I was working on Virginia Woolf's manuscripts in the New York Public Library, a friend told me, "What you've experienced sounds like what the Sufis talk about," so I read Idries Shah and tried to find a Sufi, without success. Then one day, back in Canada, someone said, "I read a book by a doctor from the United States. It sounds like he went through something just like you did."[1] She said he was coming to give a 3-day conference near Toronto, so I signed up for it on the spot.

On the first night of the weekend the man, whose name was Richard Moss, gave a talk to the assembled company. Thoughtfully and articulately, he described exactly the same sort of experience I had gone through at Cambridge. I recognised it in every word. But more than that, I could feel it in his energy and in the timbre of his voice. Like mine, his had been an experience of profound oneness, imbued with enormous energy, and like me he hadn't found it helpful to put it into any specific religious context, though he was clearly familiar with a wide range of sacred texts. But unlike me, I realised with an unspeakable pang of longing, he had stayed with his newfound awareness. Instead of trying to function in the old ways, as I had done, he had travelled the world in that tremulous state of unknowing, visiting ashrams, submitting himself to the life he found there and observing what happened when he did. Well, I tried to tell myself, he could do that. He was a medical doctor with means. But the fact remained: he had taken the years I had wanted to take to integrate the experience into his being. I could feel it in his presence, and in the depth and quality of his attention. That astonishing current lived inside him still.

I sat in the room with my emotions churning. Did he realise there was someone in the audience who had had the same experience he had, who knew exactly what he meant by the words he was using? He mentioned the possibility of private 3-minute interviews and I requested one, even though I was quaking with a tangle of feelings of love and loss and fear. When I was alone with him, I told him my story, and tried to express the pain I now felt to see that it was possible to do what he had done to maintain that state of being, rather than choose to let it go. His response, delivered not without compassion but certainly in what I considered to be a rather offhand way, was: "You lose a mother. You lose a brother. You lose a lover." And that was it. He virtually shrugged. I knew what he was saying: yes, it is terrible, but it's like any other loss. You learn to live with it.

I reeled out of the interview room and spent the rest of the weekend ping-ponging between anguish and fury. How could he say such a thing to me? How could this almost unbearable loss – the loss of the heavenly kingdom, it felt like – be considered in any way ordinary? He couldn't have understood what I was saying! But he did understand, I knew that. He just didn't seem to think it was that important. It wasn't until almost the close of the conference, aided no doubt by the expanded state we all seemed to have entered from the various practices we had undertaken (silence, dialogue, whirling, meditation) and from spending time in his energy field, that I was able to see the bigger picture more clearly.

Despite the fact that what I had experienced during those weeks at Cambridge was a deep initiation into egoless-ness, my ego had reconfigured around that very realisation in such a way as to have it make me feel special. Without even noticing, I had come to feel like one of the chosen, singled out among human beings for a taste of the divine. Not only had the experience been uniquely important, it had also made me feel uniquely important, and it was *that* conviction I needed to lose, because the fact was, *no-one was preferred*. I was engaged in exactly the same task as a great many other people: finding out how to live what I later heard him call "the downward arc", the act of bringing whatever awareness I had gleaned into my daily experience, step by painful human step. And this awareness was a demanding one. As in Rilke's striking poem, "The Archaic Torso of Apollo", there could be only one conclusion: "You must change your life."[2]

Living out that awareness required not just money, as I had at first naïvely believed, but also courage. Ongoing courage, it seemed, since life kept refusing to stand still. What this meant in my professional life was clear: I needed to leave academic life, despite the security it promised, to write, and to offer what I now knew about the creative process to whoever wanted to make use of it.

~

What this undertaking has made necessary for me, in my creative life as well as in the teaching I do, is a constant balancing and re-balancing of experience (which the ego seems all too willing to grab hold of and use to predict the future) with a kind of radical uncertainty. I have never completed an extended writing project (like a novel, or my Ph.D. thesis) without some stunning revelation that challenged everything I had thought I was undertaking, just as I seldom manage to get through a workshop without having to go through what I have come to think of as a "door" – some major moment of uncertainty that calls on a skill I seem not yet to have developed or a risk I never thought I would have to take. (If I say to myself, "Okay, this is the door," it helps me – such a little, familiar phrase to wave in the face of such a yawning unknown.)

So, in writing as in life, I keep the door open to unknowing in whatever ways present themselves, and that also means honouring what arises in that way, however challenging that may be. There are times when doing so seems absolutely pointless – times, in other words, when the powerfully habitual "intending" part of my mind has the upper hand.

Fortunately, at times like these, the words of one of my students often come back to me: "Whenever I get stuck," she said, "I tell myself, 'Just go back to the precepts.'" Honour what comes up for you, that is to say, and try not to second-guess yourself. Make the most resonant choice available to you in the moment (or failing that, "go fearward"), taking into account the situation in which you find yourself. The more often I do this, the more strongly my experience shows me that doing this will work, and that life will come to meet me in some way. Even at the times when none of this seems to work, I can know that I've done my best. I've accepted whatever risks the task or the situation presented to me, and not allowed my writing, or my life, to stultify.

Let us begin, then, with a closer look at how the fundamental precepts of Freefall Writing will continue to serve you as you take your writing forward.

Chapter Two

The Precepts Revisited

Come what may, the five precepts of Freefall Writing will always provide the fundamental guidance for your writing journey. But with time and familiarity, certain expectations can develop that don't belong to them. So however well you may believe you know them by now, it might be a good idea to take a closer look at what they are actually telling you.

1. *Write what comes up for you*
No matter what genre you choose to write in, this precept will always remain at the core of your writing life. The honouring of what arises for you *as* you write is your life-source as a writer, the wellspring of your creativity. No matter what kind of writing you aspire to, *writing is always going to be a voyage of discovery*. And this fact holds true *even in revision*.

One thing this means is that your writing can't be limited by your expectations, not even by expectations based on what's happened for you previously in Freefall. It's "what comes up for you" not "what has come up for you before".

So even though, for example, the autobiographical impulse may have come up every time you wrote and taken you a very long way in Freefall, you must be willing to let that expectation go. The central importance of the untrammeled freedom to discover lies at the very heart of this precept.

2. *Don't change anything*
At the stage of initial discovery, as your material first arises, it is imperative that you bear in mind this precept. Without first learning to honour what comes up for you, in exactly the way it comes up for you, you will never

fully learn to trust your writing voice, let alone discover what a vast store of writing skills you already possess. This precept will always be of crucial importance to you in the act of writing, whenever new material is required.

3. Go where the energy is, or go fearward

This precept is both an amplification of #1, and a practical guide to finding your place within it. It suggests that you turn towards what has energy for you. As you know by now, that energy – or if you can't find the energy, fear – often signals where your most powerful material lies.

What may not be quite so obvious is that that energy – or fear – also signals whatever constitutes the growing edge for you as writer. By now, that edge may not lie primarily in the material itself for you, but rather in the demands of the form. It may, for instance, flare up on the boundary, or what you see as the boundary, between autobiography and invention. Or it may come up when the writing seems to demand that you try a new technique you don't yet know if you can handle. Wherever you experience it, there is one guarantee: if you keep facing into the energy you can sense among the choices that present themselves, if you keep "going fearward", whatever that may turn out to mean, the scope of your writing will continue to expand.

4. Give all the sensuous details

By following this precept, you have learned to open up the writing and "show" what you might otherwise have been content to "tell" or summarise. This is one of the central skills you have acquired through the practice of Freefall Writing: to give the specific, sensuous details of how things taste, look, smell, feel and sound (including what people are saying) in the world you are writing about.

The ability to become present for those details in the moment of the act of writing is a skill you will always need to draw on, no matter in what direction you decide to take your writing. But if you are in the process of making the shift to fiction or memoir, it's worth reflecting on one of the hidden strengths you've already developed as a writer through this precept. To whatever extent you have been giving "all the sensuous details", *you have always been inventing*, stating what you imagine would have been the case, given what you already know.

No-one "remembers" the degree of detail your writing has required. You've landed in a scene, looked around, and "found" those details, which your imagination supplied. (That's why I say I consider "I don't remember" to be an editorial comment. Nobody remembers all that they're showing. You "just say" or, in other words, make up what you need. You may come to believe afterward that what you wrote is all true, and is "what happened", but that's another story.) If your goal is to write memoir, it's good to realise that you're already doing what all good memoir-writers must do, to bring their worlds alive. And if your goal is fiction, it helps to know that this will not require you to take an entirely new step, but simply a further one, in that you'll continue to employ the skills of invention you have already shown you possess.

5. Remember the "Ten-Year Rule"

Through this precept, you opened up the space of possibility between you and any autobiographical material that arose for you in Freefall. The passage of this much time usually means that you will have gained some distance from that material. And with that distance, it will have become possible for you both to identify with the character (or past self) who had that experience, and also to write about it. That dual perspective, through which you can share a character's point of view but at the same time function competently as the narrator of that character's story, is one of the most important skills a fiction- or memoir-writer can possess. And you have already learned that skill, even if largely unconsciously, by invoking the "Ten-Year Rule".

What you will be doing now, if your aim is to write fiction, is to bring that same skill to the service of a character who may embody, for instance, only one aspect of you, or none, along with aspects of other people you know or people you have never known. Whatever it is that connects you to this character will allow you to sink into him or her in the same way you did for your own past selves, and with the same degree of empathy, even as you function as the narrator who writes that character's story.

Even if it is not your goal to write fiction, this precept will already have taught you a great deal about objectivity, placing you well along the path of discovering the essence of your story (the subject of Chapter Three). Memoir and even poetry will demand this ability from you, as will any type of non-fiction that makes use of autobiographical material. In any of these genres, you will find it enormously helpful to bear in mind the "Ten-Year Rule".

And there is a new precept on the horizon which will eventually come into play. Although it only applies in revision – the subject of Chapter Twelve – I include it here because it touches on the vast open space of potential that lies behind all the other precepts as well: the awareness that your own creativity can be relied on to continue to furnish what you need.

6. Change anything

When you're coming up with new material, it's important that you remember the second precept ("Don't change anything"). However, when you're revising previously-written material, the opposite applies. You need to be willing to approach that writing with no attachment to the actual words you used before. "Don't think of words when you stop," as Jack Kerouac advised in his "List of Essentials", "but to see picture better".[3] Change *anything*. It's not what you said before that counts; it's what you are showing.

At first, when I approached a piece of my Freefall Writing someone had praised in the past, I used to stare at it and think, "How can I touch it? What if I change the very thing that worked for that person in the first place?" Not surprisingly, I found it a huge relief to let that notion go. The truth is, of course, that whatever brought the words we used in the first place will now bring whatever words are needed in this new context. And that will happen over and over again.

Keep this precept in reserve for when the time comes to re-write something you have already written. But let it shine its light into other dark corners, too. It offers fundamental reassurance about the process you are engaged in – the unending resources that are available for you to draw on, and the bounty of this act of writing in which we are all engaged.

~

Held in this wider context of understanding, the Freefall Writing precepts will continue to serve you. Freed from any of the expectations that may have crystallised around them as you wrote, they will provide a touchstone for you to come back to again and again, throughout this next phase of your writing life.

Chapter Three
Finding the Essence

To have a sense, however intuitively, of what constitutes the core of something you are writing (or have already written) allows you to move from the completely unplanned progression of Freefall to one in which all parts contribute to the whole. That insight into what I call the "essence" of a piece of writing may simply arise unbidden: before you write something, during the writing, or when you look back at it (usually after a certain amount of time has passed). But with such an insight often comes a sense of what form this writing could ultimately take: that of a short story, novel, memoir, poem or reflection, for example.

Some writers arrive at this sort of discovery, apparently, by standing back and asking themselves, "What is this piece of writing (going to be) about?" and, "What form should it take?" But for many writers – and I suspect most Freefall writers number among them – that knowing arises much more intuitively, often in the course of writing.

In this chapter, I would like to discuss some of the typical ways I see such insights surface in Freefall Writing. Of course the ways you may gain insight into the essence of your work are going to be very idiosyncratic. But by reading these examples (and doing the attendant exercises), I think you may find yourself more capable of seeing how to penetrate to the core of something you've written, and more alert to the moments of comprehension that do arise as you write.

Self-Evident Potential

Sometimes when you look back at a passage of Freefall Writing, you can see that it signals quite overtly what its central concerns are, and thus its potential to be taken further. Have a look at this piece, inspired by one of my favourite timed writing topics, "A Sound Heard in Childhood". (Please note that here, as with all the Freefall Writing quoted in this book, the writing is unedited and appears as it was spontaneously written.)

A siren eeeh aaah eeeh aaah. The dormitory is cold. Windows need to be left open the rules say. Fresh air is good for young minds. I shiver. Is it the frosted air leaking under my skimpy covers or is it the sirens? I hear a door slam. Shauna sleeping next to me groans, her blond hair falls across her forehead. Is she awake? Is anyone awake? Am I the only one in the world awake to hear this sound I hate? I want to block my ears and hide from the sounds of the police. I know where they're going. To the servants' quarters to round them up and take them away. Passbooks stay; no passbooks go to jail. I feel so cold. What about Elliot and his shining eyes? "Finished your porridge, mam?" he asks me at breakfast. He's shy and I feel it. He's scared. He's from Rhodesia – no passbook. Please God don't let them take him to jail. He's kind and good and won't harm anyone. Please God help him hide from the police. Help him to be in the dining room tomorrow morning. His wife and baby are back home. His son Joshua is a smiling baby with dimples in his cheeks and a smiling face like his dad. I hear people's voices.

"Shauna," I call softly. "Wake up they're taking Elliot. We've got to help him." I'm sweating and shaking. I don't know how to help. I hear shouting. Many voices coming from the compound. Doors of a van slam shut. Cars rev up into the night. Then silence. Everything is quiet but noisy at the same time. Everything's the same but nothing's the same. Hot and cold. Sweaty sheets stick to me. I'm such a coward. I should have gone down there. I should have hit those policemen. Screamed at them to let Elliot alone. Screamed at them to leave.

"Shauna are you still sleeping?"
(Merle Levin)

As a piece of writing, this seems to me quite perfect in itself: a gripping evocation of the experience of apartheid, seen through a white child's eyes. But what this writer is showing here clearly has the capacity to be taken further – into a short story, or perhaps even a novel.

It concerns a child who is born into the dominant (white) culture, but who also experiences herself as an outsider (or so I infer from the fact that she's the only one who seems to hear the sirens, from her empathy with Elliot, and perhaps above all from the sentence, "He's shy and I feel it"). Shauna, sleeping so soundly in the next bed, appears not to be troubled by such feelings of difference. Could this I-character's own story be developed in such a way that it reflects and is reflected in the apartheid story? Does it feel big enough (as in, compelling enough to the author) to grow into a novel? Or should it remain a short story, centred on this one incident? Its author would have to write her way into it further, to see.

This achingly beautiful little passage by Frances Arnett Sbrocchi also announces its own essence clearly, though in a very different way:

An hour to be young again, to sing from here to Nannup, to walk along the river, watch the circles drift under the shadows, to hear the gum nuts dropping, making more centres, trust the heron, the blue heron who, statue-still, is watching. To drift through days of gentleness, long nights of tender talk to walk in silence where unseen watchers know our loving keeps us safe. For we are gentled with the wonder, our wanderings along known trails. There is no longer reason for striving, or for winning – we have each other and we need nothing. Take my hand darling as we climb to the wooden bridge – no trains run along this track. It ends but a mile beyond the further shore.

This is already a complete prose-poem about love, seen from the perspective of age. But its lyrical tone and graceful use of metaphor immediately suggest too that the same felt-sense of love could be conveyed in a poem. For me, as an inveterate lover of stories, it opens up channels in other directions as well. The way the past and present, the known and the unknown, play like dappled sunshine over the actions of the couple hints at some new kind of kaleidoscopic story-structure that could extend the action far beyond the confines of this one shared walk. Could this passage stand at the end of a saga of struggle, shown against a backdrop this alive, this filled with spirit? Too fanciful? However, it could be. This is the exciting time, when everything is possible.

Potential Unveiled

Writing is a voyage of discovery. It brings you things you did not have in mind when you started. Sometimes just following a hunch that arises as you write, or noticing the desire to go back to something you thought was finished and write more, can lead you to a whole new sense of what that piece of writing is about.

Here are some excerpts from a piece which shows that, despite what a writer may *intend* to write about, deeper potential can emerge through the act of writing. Katharina Rout, a gifted translator now living in Canada, grew up in a large family in Germany in which the father was a pastor. "What got me started with the piece," she says, "was a conversation with Jonathan [her husband]. I was telling him how we always had to sing in the car and how I ended up hating it. Write about it, he said."

Accordingly, she starts well back in childhood when, after two church services, the mother serves the Sunday lunch. The children, having helped each parent in turn during the long morning, are looking forward to their one meat meal of the week. But before they can even say grace, the father says, "Let's have a song, Gertrud":

Mother, who was a trained choir leader, started singing: "Praise to the Lord the Almighty, the King of Creation". We sang its five stanzas while the steam rising from the cauliflower disappeared and the white sauce began to form a skin. At least she had not chosen "Rise, My Soul, and Sing" which had ten stanzas or, worse still, "Go and Find Your Joy, O Heart" which had a staggering fifteen stanzas we knew by heart. It was all right to sing that one in the car, and we often did, but before lunch, it was not one of our favourites.

"That was so lovely, let's have another one," Father said, just when we hoped he would start to pray.

In this way, the battle lines are drawn. The narrator pits Mother (whose knowledge of music is quite profound) against Father (who lustily embraces the religious aspect of the music) and places herself (the I-character) between them.

Years later, as a teenager, I suffered through the hymns and canons, the prayers, and the hand-holding with growing outrage. How can Father treat Mother's work with such disrespect? Cut him short, I demanded. Make him honour woman's labour. But Mother claimed she enjoyed the singing and did not care one bit if her food got cold. I was furious. Not only was my father a patriarch of biblical proportions, my mother perfectly matched the cliché of the meek little woman, devoted to the proverbial three K's: Kinder, Küche, Kirche – her children, her kitchen, her church. What chance did I stand of ever being emancipated with parents like this?

The older she gets, the more lance-like her protests:

I heard they sang this in the Hitler Youth, I said one day just when we were about to sing my brother's request, "Wild Geese are Rushing Through the Night." Rubbish, Mother said, that song is much older. Your grandfather could tell you how they already sang it in the German Youth Movement. So? I asked as sarcastically as I could. Well, she said, the Youth Movement was all idealistic and romantic and very moral. I should have thought you'd feel a kinship with their protest against authority, she said. I turned to Father: Did you, or did you not, sing this song in the Wehrmacht? He sighed. They made us sing all sorts of songs just to keep us marching, he said. We were so tired. We could not have marched those long days had it not been for the songs. Right, I triumphed. Just like you make us sing when we're on holiday in Austria and are too tired to walk down the mountain! Why don't we sing your brother's song now, Mother suggested. I don't want to sing a Nazi song, I said and looked at my brother to make him feel ashamed of his choice. The Falcons sing "Wild Geese" to this day, Father said, obviously assuming that whatever the Socialist Youth Association sang would be fine with me. And so does the Bundeswehr, I countered.

By the end of the Freefall, she concludes, "We groaned when we heard Father's 'Let's have a song' until he no longer suggested it. [...] We were sick of singing."

With that statement, Katharina had clearly completed the task she set herself: to write about singing in the car, and how she ended up hating it. But she reports that the next day, even though she had "no sense of its being incomplete", she found herself returning to the piece to write several paragraphs about the mother's subsequent illness with thyroid cancer. In those we see how, when the mother's vocal chords are about to be cut in an operation, the family returns to singing: "We all met at our parents' house. We sat around the Advent wreath, lit its candles, and opened our scores. Fighting back tears, we sang the chorales of Bach's *Christmas Oratory* for a last time." Sometime after the operation, the mother becomes able, against all odds, to sing again. Astonishingly, the doctor later discovers, she has "trained her one [remaining] chord to vibrate and close against the side of her voice box. A miracle!" From then on, "before each of her operations, we sang." Still later, when the mother has died and the father is mute with grief, the children know how to respond. "We looked for the scores. We struggled. But we made it again through the chorales of Bach's *Christmas Oratory*."

For me, these final paragraphs bring out a different thread entirely than in the earlier pages, and one the writer herself may not have been aware of when they were written. Given the power of this new ending, we can see the mother's real triumph, and realise that that too has been evolving from the outset. While the daughter argued feminism, or the children grew tired, as children do, of each phase of the singing, their mother used her intelligence and knowledge of music to keep them at it, and to keep her own life – and theirs – in a certain kind of harmony. Through singing, she kept an overbearing husband and a rebellious family united for as long as she could, and left it with a sense of itself *as* a family, still infused with the values (intelligence, individuality, and a love of something higher) that were closest to her heart. Singing, you could almost say, was her own brand of feminism, and a deeper and more capacious one than any that her eldest daughter, the I-character, had yet discovered.

For Freefall writers, to stay open to the way a new kind of significance can emerge over the course of writing "what comes up" in a particular subject area is important. This particular thread might or might not turn out to be what engages Katharina most deeply in the piece she has written. But you can see how a central concern like this would shift the focus from a chain of historical events that led to an attitude ("I grew to hate it") on the part of the I-character to the more subtle exposition of a deeper truth about humanity. A focus such as this could well lead to the piece being subtly disengaged from its dependence on "what happened" in life, to become a self-consistent, internally-resonant whole more suited to that purpose, *even though this might not mean changing very much.*

Possibility Opened Out

The "opening out" technique I described in *Writing Without a Parachute* can also prove a way of gaining insight into the core or essence of a piece of writing. Opening out, as you may recall, means going back into a sentence from a piece of Freefall you've already written and re-entering that world at that point, with a view to showing what happens moment by moment in whatever scene you find there. When I ask a writer to "open out" a sentence, it's because that sentence has energy for me, which is, I suppose, a way of saying that I have a hunch that something of significance for the piece, or for the writer's relationship to writing, may emerge from doing so. But when you've left a piece of Freefall alone for a while, you can often do this for yourself when you read it over. Is there something you've summarised because you wanted to avoid going into it? (There's energy there.) Did you skim over something because you weren't sure you could handle where it would take you, either emotionally or technically? Did you satisfy yourself with merely telling something rather than showing it, because you just didn't want to get that close?

In this piece of Freefall by Rashida Murphy, there was one particular thing that pulled at me to get closer:

His name was Sohrab and he came from Shiraz. He had never heard of a wine called Shiraz because his religion forbade him to drink wine. But a few months in the company of my brothers and cousins changed that.

Sohrab spoke of his hometown with its blue domes and tiled arches and large squares and tree-lined avenues. The moon-patterned courtyards of his beloved Shiraz were so different from the dusty little village he found us in.

"Town," I reminded him. "This is a town. Officially. Soon we will be a city."

"Town, huh! This is a village and you are all villagers. And soon I will go to Amrika and study at Stanford." But that was later, once he'd learned sufficient English to insult us.

It didn't take him long to get used to us; my brothers and cousins and uncles and aunties and parents. He had a large family too, back in his crimson city that shared its name with the liquid my brothers were so fond of. My twin sister and I were the youngest and when he practised his hesitant English on us we tried not to laugh.

We lived in a remote North Indian village that had been elevated to the status of a "college town", because of the abundance of colleges run by Jesuit priests and Spanish nuns. Dark-bearded boys from Iran and Palestine had started trickling in to live and study here because it was cheaper than going to Stanford. They didn't speak to each other – the Iranians and the Palestinians – they shared a religion but not a language. They dressed better than the Indian boys and paid rent on time. For several months we had four boys sharing two rooms in our house.

When Sohrab first came he was just another curly-haired boy with thick spectacles and a funny accent. He wore stiff white shirts and round, brown moccasins that were too big for him. His eyes were huge behind those glasses. The heavy frames left dents on either side of his nose when he took them off. He polished those glasses constantly. He was blind without them and he put them on as soon as he got up in the morning. Once I found him fast asleep, after a night out with my brothers, with his glasses on. I teased him about it the next morning and he said, "I can see my dreams better if I sleep with my glasses on," with such seriousness I didn't know if he was pulling my leg. It was hard to tell with Sohrab.

Then there was the moon. He had a relationship with it. Even sober, he behaved strangely when the moon was full. He giggled and sat on the verandah with a cigarette <u>so he could look at the moon and talk to it</u>.

My mother tried to feed him constantly, especially after the revolution, when she knew he had lost his family. Lost. As if they were misplaced or hiding somewhere and would come out after the Ayatollahs won the battle against Saddam. Sohrab cried at night in his sleep and his glasses were streaked in the morning. My mother hired holy men to exorcise the evil that surrounded him and instructed us all to say prayers in a language we didn't understand. [...]

It was the phrase, "so he could look at the moon and talk to it" that intrigued me. The writer seems to have taken up a habitual distance quite far back from Sohrab, even though he is obviously an object of fascination for the child. We have a couple of sentences of dialogue, and his joke (if it is a joke) about seeing his dreams better, but the rest sits somewhere between showing and telling. But this compelling character is someone who is trying hard to adapt to the entirely different culture in which he finds himself. And he will lose his whole family, who stayed behind. Would opening out that sentence show us more about who he is, and how he handles this deep alienation? Would it bring us closer to him?

Asked to do so, Rashida wrote:

"Cancer," my sister said. "He was born in July, under the sign of Cancer. That's why he's a bit loony." And we looked at him sitting on the roof with a bottle of London Pilsner beside him, blowing smoke rings into the air. My father threatened to shoot him with an air gun if he didn't come down. The aunties muttered that he was definitely "touched" and kept their prepubescent girls away from him.

Another time he lay down on the dark gravel path outside our house and my brother nearly ran him over with his blue Lambretta. "What's the matter with you, you idiot," my brother yelled when Sohrab lay motionless on the dirt, looking upwards, as if hypnotised.

Sohrab patted the ground beside him and invited my brother to lie down. "Look, he said. "Just look. It's moving. It's getting closer to us and if we keep looking, it will come for us. And we can go to it. Don't you see?"

My brother didn't want to share a room with him after that and my father said, "Well, he can't sleep with the girls, can he now? You know what foreigners are like. This one's a little mad. So what? Just ignore him."

For me, this opened-out section does bring Sohrab closer, and it also brings to the surface the questions that point to the essence of the piece. Is Sohrab mad? Or is he trying to endure more than can be endured? In talking to the moon, is he connecting with something that makes it possible for him to hold himself together?

Later on in the original Freefall, when the I-character sees him six years later, Sohrab is blind (it's not that he can't see, the doctor says; he doesn't want to) and dying. As she lists to herself the things she can do to keep him (as the doctor suggests) comfortable, the mere mention of that image now brings these questions back again:

Don't talk about his dead sister and mother or his father and brothers. Don't remind him of his domed city with rubble in its squares and guns in its mosques. Don't speak his language. Don't tell him that he will die far from home, among people who cannot purify his spirit forty days after his body has been buried on an alien shore. Ask him if his dreams are blurred. Ask him if the moon still speaks to him.

Although it's not my purpose in asking someone to open out a sentence that they use the new piece as part of the old one, Rashida did just that, and she has now published the short story that resulted, with a few more tweaks, under the title, "The Moon Still Speaks".

Writing Experience

FREEFALL WRITING: FINDING MEANING

Take some of your earlier Freefall Writing and see if the essence of what you were writing jumps out at you. If so, take note of that, and of how it suggests you might take it further. If not, when you find particular spots that have energy for you, try Freefalling in there some more and see what emerges.

Writing Tip: When other people make suggestions about where to go with your writing, the sense of recognition is probably your most useful tool. Don't be drawn off course by suggestions that don't spark it. But when someone does suggest something you already seem to know, pay attention. That kind of awareness comes from the same place that writing comes from, and it's as good a guide as any to what's important for you there.

TIMED WRITING: WILL AND SURRENDER

As you move into this new phase of your writing, a key dynamic will be the interplay between will and surrender. The following exercises are designed to help you explore this territory in a time-limited setting, by bringing will or intention into an otherwise spontaneous piece of writing. They're also designed to help you let go of or transmute the autobiographical pull of some of your material. You may not like doing this at first. However, for ten minutes at a time, it's well worth giving it a try.

    1. "A sound heard in childhood", *redux*.
        a. First, explore this topic in the present tense, as experienced by the child.
        b. Now write the same memory in the past tense, from the perspective of the adult that child has become.

2. Pick a colour, a day of the week, a piece of fruit, and a job. Now, write about the first time you made love, and make sure to include all of your four choices. (This one is based on a suggestion from Natalie Goldberg.)

3.

a. Write on the topic, "The Same Old Argument" (in dialogue), using an argument between a parent and a child.
b. Now write that same argument as if it were occurring between partners.
c. Now write the same argument between two heads of state, on the eve of an invasion.

4.

a. Write a list of the most unusual jobs you've ever done.
b. Now choose one of those jobs, and write on the topic, "Like Mother [or Father], Like Child". Write it in the first person (as offspring) and make it as intensely personal as possible.
c. Write on the same topic, this time from the mother's [or father's] point of view.

Chapter Four
Character, Conflict and Trouble

I t's perhaps not surprising that so many Freefall writers, when they follow the first precept, find that "what comes up" for them is, at least at first, autobiographical. As Canadian novelist, Elizabeth Hay, reflected in an interview, "I think probably everybody does, because it's what is most pressing, meaningful and urgent."[4] But, as she goes on to point out, the shift into fiction demands something different, because "In fiction there is more room. In fiction you can come up with an answer whereas real life is more complicated." What fiction requires of any writer who begins with autobiographical material is an internal shift with regard to that material. Once the writer has made that shift, a vastly wider range of choices becomes available.

Nobel prize-winning short-story writer, Alice Munro, gives an excellent illustration of what this shift feels like on the inside:

There's a difference between the person and writer. The person that I am, living in a house across from a beautiful wood, would get upset when the bulldozers came in and knocked all the trees down and put up a Texaco station. The person would hate to see that such things were happening in the world. But the writer wouldn't mind at all. The writer would start watching what went on at the Texaco station.5

This curiosity and detachment, this stance of witnessing rather than reacting, frees up the events of life to achieve a wholly new kind of potential within a work of art. Before I began to write, I marvelled at the way Tom Thomson, father of the Canadian "Group of Seven" artists, could paint the deep forests of Algonquin in such transcendent detail, and then go on to paint some of those same locations as treeless wastelands after they had been completely logged, with the same degree of inspired presence. The experience of writing has made that ability much easier to comprehend. However much the person may have loved and sought out those woods, the artist is simply curious. To use Elizabeth Hay's phrase, he has more room.

Fortunately, for writers with experience in Freefall Writing, this shift is not an entirely new development. The whole purpose of the fifth Freefall precept, the "Ten-Year Rule", is to create some separation between the writer and their experience, so that the autobiographical material that does come up can be used with real benefit for learning to write. With the passage of ten years, most writers can witness their own past experience with some detachment but are nonetheless still capable of identifying with the character who had that experience. What the shift to fiction requires is a further expansion of that same capacity for detachment.

Character

When I write fiction, I find I start by becoming curious about the characters who have already presented themselves. They may be based on people I've known, or they may feature parts of people I've known somewhere in their makeup. If that is the case, my job now seems to be to get to know them from the inside, something that my own agenda, whatever it might have been, has probably prevented me from doing in life. Quite quickly, I get to know them better – much better – than I ever presumed to know them in actuality. As I write what they do, I begin to see what lies behind their actions, what drives them to act that way, and therefore what I can imagine them doing next.

All of this is governed at some level by an insight into the essence of what I want to write (for me, it's usually a novel). "Can you escape yourself?" was a question that arose for me in Freefall before I began to write a novel I set in Nigeria. This might be as particular a sense of what I want to explore in a novel as I get. My notion of what the arc of action will look like may be equally vague (in this instance it was simply this: the main character goes to Africa to escape a painful relationship breakup; in the end, she either leaves or stays). But the people in my pages – often some of the same, or combinations of the same, people who have appeared in my Freefall pages – can now let me know (if only from one page to the next) how it will play out, and at some point why. I can depend on them for that.

Some writers talk of inventing a history for their characters, or finding a telling spark and fanning it into life. But for me, as for many Freefall writers, the process tends to work the other way around. Rather than inventing a lifelike form to cloak some pre-determined motivation, I will probably have to detach myself enough from the ways I knew someone in life to understand what motivates them in my story. One good place to begin that process is to look at the direction their feet are pointing: to see what they do, and to infer from that what motives lie behind those actions. For me, however, the process is less abstract than that. I have the sense of stepping inside those footsteps – asking myself why I would have done that, so I can know how what they want feels. In this way, bits of myself may be scattered throughout the characters, but it doesn't feel that way. It feels as if I'm now really seeing them for the very first time.

Karimu, one of the central characters in that Nigerian novel, is loosely based on someone I once knew and liked very much. I was party to some of his lofty ideals, and I knew he was something of a rebel. As the story began to show itself on the page, I realised that I knew the role of a rebel quite well. I knew that edgy feeling of restlessness, of frustration with life as it stands. I knew how easy it was to lose myself in a sense of righteousness about what I deemed to be a higher cause (what the Buddhists call "attachment to views"). But the character Karimu is an African Muslim, and I don't know anything about how it is to be a man in a Muslim society, or how it is to fall in love with a white woman from a Christian country. *Does* he fall in love? Or is that all just part of the rebellion? Those things he had to show me himself, as the story developed. Those things I had to write my way into, to see.

Conflict

When I wrote that novel, I was determined to write it by Freefall Writing principles: writing what came up for me, trying not to change anything, giving all the sensuous detail, going where there was energy as I wrote. I set my characters in motion, and honoured what came up for them.

Apart from that first glimpse of the question I wanted to explore, which arrived along with the understanding that what I wanted to write *was* a novel, I had no overall concept of what would happen. I simply stayed with the characters and found out what they did. This felt like a matter of necessity rather than choice. I knew that if I backed off to analyse what I was doing, all my skills in self-criticism would find their way in, and I wouldn't be able to write it at all. As long as I stayed with the characters, that didn't happen. But I soon discovered that while some scenes seemed to go well and have a certain zing to them, others fell utterly flat. And I had no idea why.

Finally, after trying to write one particular scene for about two weeks without success, I found out why it fell so flat. The main character, fleeing the torture of jealousy over her partner's affair with her good friend in Scotland, had taken a job as far away as possible, in a small town in Nigeria. In this scene, she was experiencing life in a tribal village for the first time. But although dusk had fallen and the cooking fires were burning, packs of naked children were running around, and the women were pounding yam for all they were worth, nothing was happening. I felt as if I were writing a travelogue. Flat, flat, flat. Day after day I returned to it, feeling like a chicken scratching dry earth, and still nothing happened. Then from the door of one of the huts emerged Grace, a lovely woman and the soul of kindness, the youngest wife of the elderly village chief. And Grace, it turned out, was also close friends with Karimu, the man with whom the main character had begun, slowly and reluctantly, to form a relationship. With that, the demon Jealousy was back. All of a sudden, the scene had life.

What I discovered in that scene was the importance of conflict. Doubtless other major scenes I had written contained conflict, but I hadn't recognised it as the vital element it was. Here, where it took so long to arise, I could see it. Someone wants something (Sarah, the main character, wants to pursue this new relationship) and an obstacle (she perceives Grace as an obstacle) stands in the way of that desire. Tension builds as Sarah discovers – or projects – just how much of an obstacle Grace is going to be. And that conflict, with its attendant tension, gives the scene life.

As the scene ends, that tension is relieved by Grace's thoughtfulness and by Karimu's ongoing attentions. But doubts creep in. Yes, Sarah is feeling better, but is the problem really solved? Is she ever going to be able come to grips with a polygamous society? Or herself? I could feel that this particular vector of conflict was only going to intensify as the novel unfolded.

In other words, nothing much has changed since Aristotle, who showed in the *Poetics* how conflict escalates to an appropriate climax and is then resolved in the concluding action of a play[6]. There are those who would argue that this pattern will be reflected in every part of the story, even at the level of the individual scene – as I discovered in this one. That slow-sided wedge of difficulties that build to a climax and then fall away seems to be as natural to us as breathing (and is, perhaps, as natural as sex).

If I had held the intention to *produce* this sort of build-up, this rise and fall, in the forefront of my mind, I could probably never have written this scene. To get there, I had to follow the characters and see what they did. Yet I could certainly tell when it wasn't happening, and that I had to keep digging to get somewhere. I had to honour my own internal balance, in other words, between intention and surrender, in order to move forward.

Trouble

Why trouble seems to be so important to any work of fiction, be it a play, a short story, or a novel, and arguably, to memoir and poetry as well, is a question I often see writers ponder. As dearly as many of us would like to write stories where things go from good to better, when we try – as I tried at first, in the scene I have described – it just doesn't work. When British novelist Ian McEwan was asked in a radio interview why fiction so routinely portrays difficulty in relationships, he put it this way: "It's only when a couple is unhappy that there's anything to write about. When two people are happy together, there's just white space."

Anyone who has done Freefall Writing will have had direct experience of the difference between writing "fearward" and not doing so. Writing what you don't want to write has the power to grip you, and the ability to surrender to the writing is just one of the gifts that that kind of absorption can bring. But can that be the only reason so many forms of writing revolve around difficulty? The writer's own desire to be gripped by what he or she is doing?

I think of *Romeo and Juliet*, or *King Lear*, and the fact that for their protagonists, just when everything seems to be going well, that's just the time for something new to pop up from the shadow to be dealt with: "now I think I'll fall in love with someone from a family my parents hate", or "now I need to see which of my daughters loves me most". Very often this is something that they may not have had the security or psychic space to attempt before. The trouble that these decisions give rise to is the seat of tragedy, yes, but if it's not too big a stretch to make the comparison, just as "going fearward" often opens up new territory for us as writers, so these troublesome decisions also open up the possibility of something larger, some insight into life (either for them or for the audience) that these characters were previously denied. Perhaps that's why all writers find themselves doing the same for their characters. They give them trouble, and take them to that "fearward" edge – the growing edge, where something can be confronted that couldn't be faced before. Something that takes them further into their incarnation as human beings.

In the next two chapters, I'll be looking more deeply at some of the ways characters evolve and plots form. But as you think about or, preferably, write your way into these things, this point is worth bearing in mind: those characters are going to want things, and that wanting is going to get them into trouble. Without that, it's going to be hard for them, or their story, to grow.

Writing Experience

FREEFALL WRITING: DISCOVERING MOTIVATION

Throughout this month, keep writing Freefall that "goes fearward". Whatever that might mean for you, dig in. Looking back, become aware of the nature and degree of conflict in the scenes that that writing generates.

If you've found stories or scenes in your earlier Freefall that compel you, have a look at what your main, or point-of-view, character is doing there. Infer from those actions what that character wants. Think about the motives that might have given rise to those goals. Could you show some of those motives operating in a scene from that character's past? Try freefalling a couple.

Given his or her motives, what might the character do next? Freefall a scene based on your hunch, but include someone who tries to stop your character from doing it. Now freefall that scene from that other character's (the antagonist's) viewpoint. Finally, freefall a third scene from the main character's viewpoint, where that wanting is intensified.

Writing Tip: What you write from the antagonist's point of view doesn't have to be great literature. The important thing is to get some practice in feeling what an antagonist wants, as a means of opening up the field in which you experience motivation.

TIMED WRITING: CONFLICT AND CHARACTER

Use these and similar topics of your own invention to give you immediate experience in writing about conflict. As always in the timed writings, let the topic take you to a particular scene you can show, rather than to a meditation on the topic in general. (Ten minutes will be enough.)

1. No way out
2. Trying to win
3. Telling a lie
4. Waiting
5. Making a mistake
6. Lost!
7. Unfair
8. What's love got to do with it?
9. The person I lived in terror of was X (Remember to take this into a specific scene)

Now, if one or more of these topics generates both a character who wants something, and a character who is trying to prevent her or him from getting it:

a. Consider what your protagonist wanted in that scene. What does that suggest to you her or his conscious goal might be? Unconscious goal? Can you suggest a reason he or she might have that goal?

b. Consider what the antagonist's motivation might be for trying to prevent your character from achieving that goal. What does that suggest about the antagonist's goal or goals? What might be a reason she or he has developed that goal?

c. Write the same scene from the antagonist's point of view.

Writing Tip: Occasionally, I come across someone who habitually allows whatever tension arises in the writing to flatten out or trail off before the situation can come to a head. (If you're uncertain whether you have this problem, look back at the previous chapter's "same old argument" pieces. If the arguments petered out, or reached a resolution in which one person capitulated to the other, read on.)

Since the ability to sustain and build tension is essential to most fiction, try this: think of something you deeply want or have wanted, and have been prevented from having. Give yourself a writing topic related to that desire (i.e. give me that; keep your hands off my child/wife/husband; stop torturing that puppy/kitten/child; leave me alone; if I had it to do over!) and write the scene that emerges from that topic. Experience the feeling of strong wanting in as many writing situations (scenes) as possible. Now, look back at the scenes where someone in particular has prevented the character you identify with from getting what she or he wants. What do you think that person wants? Write the scene from that character's point of view, allowing him or her to want just as badly. That feeling is the place to start.

Don't forget the Freefall Writing precepts: write what comes up for you; don't change anything; give all the sensuous details; go fearward; remember the "Ten-Year Rule".

Chapter Five
Inhabiting Character

When you're writing fiction, and even in certain kinds of non-fiction, there comes a point when the characters in your story begin to get up and walk around on their own. The balance you've been maintaining between intention and surrender shifts. You no longer have to propel them along as much; they take their own initiative. Choosing characters who take an active role in their own destiny is a big help. Confronting them with difficulties, the element of "trouble" discussed in the previous chapter, hastens this change. But nothing helps as much as does your knowing them, inside and out. Once you've spent enough time with them to see what they do, and to gain an understanding of why they do it, they seem to become self-sustaining, and the story begins to feel as if it writes itself.

Opening Out

As E. M. Forster observed, characters in fiction "often seem more definite than characters in history, or even our own friends; we have been told all about them that can be told; even if they are imperfect or unreal they do not contain any secrets, whereas our friends do and must, mutual secrecy being one of the conditions of life upon this globe."[7] But getting to the point at which the characters in our stories do not keep any secrets from us often proves easier with wholly-invented characters than with those who are taken, even in part, from life. Characters we have created from the ground up are typically animated by our own self-knowledge;

they embody some aspect of ourselves. Because of this, they already feel familiar, and although we may not know what they are going to do next, when they do it, we can understand why. Characters based even in part on people we have known in life can be much more inscrutable, yet it is our job to get to know and understand them equally thoroughly. We are responsible for what they do on our pages – even if those actions turn out to be some of the very same ones they performed in life.

One of the best ways I've discovered for getting to know a character who has already appeared in Freefall is through the same sort of "opening out" process you may have used to help discover the story's essence.

This is how it works for understanding character. When you come to a place in your Freefall Writing where a character you'd like to understand better has done something that seems inexplicable to you, take twenty minutes to "open out" that place in the narrative. (A specific phrase or sentence works best.) Show whatever scene comes up for you in connection with the particular action or aspect of character pinpointed in that sentence. Don't use the writing to ponder; use it to take you there. *Writing is not the same as thinking* and if you enter it fully, it will show you very different things about that character than thinking can. Dialogue will help, as will remembering to proceed from moment to moment in whatever scene comes up for you. Bear in mind the fact that you are not trying to write something that will fit into the original piece. Your aim here is to discover whatever else comes up, in connection with that aspect of this character.

Here is an example of how "opening out" helped this writer begin to understand her character better. This is the original piece of Freefall Writing:

I woke to the sound of my father's voice. It was a tone I didn't recognize.

"So I want you to stop being so critical of me. I've had enough. It's not fair. I do the work. I earn the money. I look after you real well. Don't I?"

There was a silence and then barely audible, "You're right, Russ. You are a good person. I didn't know, I didn't realise that I was being critical."

"Well, dammit, you are. No more."

The door slammed shut.

I was stunned. My father never swore. […] My poor mother! She must be devastated. […]

Then came the sound of the car backing out of the garage. I heard a noise from the kitchen. It sounded like whimpering. God, she's crying, I thought. I curled up in bed. The noise got louder. It didn't sound like crying anymore. Suddenly I identified the noise. She was chuckling. It got louder. Then I heard a full throated laugh. I rolled over in bed and sat up to make sure I was hearing correctly. It was definitely laughter. How could she laugh? What he had said was devastating. His tone was so raw. I heard the sound of the dishwasher start.

There was no answer. How could she laugh? Maybe she hadn't really heard him. Maybe she was laughing so she wouldn't cry. Maybe she didn't give a damn. But, no, she was my mother. She was sensitive and she cared so much. But how could she laugh? I lay there. Who was this person?
(Patricia Klinck)

Who was this person indeed? That's precisely the question the writer will have to answer if she is going to become able to give the mother her freedom as a character in her story. In this piece of Freefall, the writer has evoked an engaging, enigmatic presence. But who is she? More specifically, in the context of this particular story, *why did she laugh?* To find the answer to that question (to her own satisfaction, anyway), the author needs to begin to get to know the mother as a character, better.

A good place for this writer to "open out" in her piece, therefore, is the question, "How could she laugh?" Twenty minutes' writing gave rise to the following:

It was Saturday morning. I could smell the coffee and the burnt toast. Lying in bed on the other side of the door, I could picture the kitchen table, turquoise and white with my parents sitting facing each other.

It was my mother's voice, soft, clear. "[…] Alan and I had been fighting all morning so I guess that's why Poppa took us with him. Just to give Momma a break. When we got to the pasture where the bull was [for sale], he said, 'You two just stay in the car. I've had enough of your bickering for a lifetime.'" My parents both laughed.

"He had a lot of patience, your father." […]

"Yes, well, he got over the fence and started towards the bull. Alan and I were glued to the window. Poppa just moved very slowly. I could see his mouth moving. 'Hey, Alan,' I said. 'Poppa's talking to the bull.' 'He'd better,' said Alan. 'The bull has both eyes open and on him now.'

"'Tell you what, Alan,' I said to him. 'That bull's gonna charge Poppa. I'll put money on the bull.' 'You gotta be kidding, Elizabeth,' he said. 'Have you no loyalty?' 'I've got a nickel on the bull. Wanna place your bet on Poppa?' He grinned at me, spit on his hand and we shook."

"Hee hee," laughed my father. "You bet on the bull! What a thing to do." They both laughed again. I heard my father slap his leg. [...]

"So the bull pawed the ground."

"And I'll bet George did too," my father added. Another belly laugh.

"Then Poppa turned and ran for the fence. The bull gained on him. 'Go for it Poppa,' Alan was shouting. 'C'mon, bull!' I shouted.

"The bull's horns hit the top rail just as Poppa jumped over it. It was spectacular! He stopped and looked closely at the bull. Slowly he came over and sat in the car. I could hear him panting.

"'So that makes five cents,' I said as I counted the last penny into Alan's hand. 'What are you two up to?' Poppa asked. 'Well, I'm just paying him the bet we made,' I explained. 'Alan bet on you, Poppa, and I bet on the bull.'

"Poppa just turned and looked into the back seat. 'Elizabeth,' he said, 'I am real disappointed in you. That bull could've killed me.' 'But he didn't and you sure have great running style.'

"I saw his ears go red – which wasn't a good sign. But he didn't say a word. He just started up the old Ford and we drove back home, really slow."

As often happens with "opening out" pieces, this one goes sideways, as it were, from the original Freefall Writing. Rather than providing an explanation of the mother's behaviour in the first piece, it gives another, more intimate experience of this aspect of the mother's behaviour, by means of which we begin to understand it better. There is clearly something quite unique about her sense of humour which, according to her own story, showed itself even in childhood. Henri Bergson suggests that laughter involves "a momentary anesthesia of the heart".[8] I think this holds true for all of us, but it seems to be especially true in her case. When something strikes her as funny, the humour predominates, even when the situation may involve a certain amount of pain on the part of another person.

For me, this insight also helps to answer another question that has been lingering from the first piece. Despite the I-character's assurances, I still wondered: how much does she really care about her husband? Now that I'm better able to grasp this characteristic, and to see how much the husband enjoys it too, I don't find myself wondering any more.

Characters Taken from Life

Since we often have to work quite hard to understand what motivates characters taken from life so that they can become viable characters on the page, the question arises, why use them at all? Why not invent all of our characters out of whole cloth instead?

For many writers, the impulse to write at all arises in large part from their desire to make sense of the world they know, and of the people in it, whether they do so in fiction, memoir or poetry. It's the world they know that "has energy" for them, to use my own terminology. The people involved may be completely transformed in the course of the writing, or they may not be, but a large part of the writer's task will probably consist of making sense of them, and of their significance in what is now being written.

It is also simply a fact that characters taken (at least in part) from life work best for many people. When these writers try to do otherwise they discover, as Thomas Merton discovered, that "I try to create some new, objective, separate person outside myself, and it doesn't work. I make some stupid, wooden guy."[9] The conclusion he came to holds true for many writers:

> *Such things I love as I love myself I can write about easier than about things that don't exist and therefore can't be loved. I guess I could write a much better short story about angels I love than about some purely fanciful person who cannot be conceived as having any of the characteristics of anyone I ever loved.*[10]

Finally, I'm just not sure that when it comes to the imagination, we have much of a choice. When someone is actually writing, it's largely down to the first precept, "what comes up", whether they've come into writing through Freefall or not. The wide-open, fertile ground of the imagination doesn't eliminate, it includes. How the known will mix with the unknown is not something you plan; it's something you discover as you write.

Working from Known to Unknown

One catch, however: even if the person your character is based on is someone you don't like in life, you will need to reach a point with that character where you can understand what motivates her or him, too. The people we don't love already, when they crop up in our writing, can present the hardest task of all. But as with any other character, if those people are to become viable on the page, understanding and even some empathy still seems to be required. Time and again, I have seen vicious, nasty characters fall flat in someone's writing, because that writer doesn't yet understand what makes them tick. Fortunately, once he or she gets to know them better, they begin to stand up and walk. *Though they may be no less villainous*, they have become explicable to their author, which releases me, as the reader, from the task I would otherwise default to: that of coming up with excuses for them in my own mind as I read.

For these and all the characters whose traits you don't feel you share, one good route into them is nonetheless to use your own self-knowledge. Suppose, for example, that one of your characters is an abusive alcoholic. While you may not have had any direct experience of that particular behaviour, you doubtless have experience of other irresistible habits and of the feeling of uncontrollable wanting that goes with them. Whether that craving is for food, cigarettes, gambling, television, reading or sex, you can draw on its emotional truth to understand how your alcoholic character feels, and to know what he or she might do as a result. Can you marry this feeling with that of abusing someone, another human behaviour of which we have all had experience one way or another? Self-knowledge is an invaluable storehouse in taking responsibility for such characters. And it must be done. On the page they are our creatures, after all.

Grasping the I-Character

Paradoxically, the character who may prove the most diffuse or difficult to comprehend may be the one whose point of view you most closely share. Though this may not literally be an I-character (unless you're writing in the first person), I use that term here to mean a character who comes close to embodying your own point of view, albeit (if you're following the "Ten-Year Rule") that of a past self.

When you find yourself working with such a character, it's easy to assume you know them well. You're consummately familiar, of course, with the ways you've thought, and how you've perceived. Yet you also know, if you're at all introspective, how seldom you've ever been aware of a clear or even conscious motive for what you've done, and how random your actions often seem to you. How do you now make such a character explicable to yourself? How do you get to know the I-character well enough in their role in this particular story to make her or him feel vivid and complete?

Here too, writing your way into the character can hold the key. Writing Freefall may already have helped you to acquire some sense of who you are, or have been, on the page, in certain situations. But you may still be too close to that character to see him or her clearly. "Opening out" something that has been glossed over in a piece may help you to shift that identification.

Watch how this happens when Australian writer, Christine Driver, opens out a sentence from her Freefall. Here is the original piece:

"Owww."

His brown legs hopped up and down. I held him tight by one skinny wrist and swung the blackboard ruler around again. There wasn't much of a noise when it connected with his backside in its baggy khaki shorts. I let him go and let the ruler drop. My hands were shaking and I felt rocky. Seven-year-old Anselm grinned,

"That hurt Miss."

I couldn't speak. The flowers on my home-made blue cotton dress were blurring as I looked at them. I'd been told the only fabric to wear in Derby was cotton. So I'd spent some of my holidays choosing fresh colours and making up lengths of soft cotton into dresses with loose waists and short sleeves. This one had a gathered skirt that billowed out when I was whacking Anselm as he ran rings around me. We were right at the edge of the classroom next to the louvres that ran down to the floor. The louvres were glass except for the last six rows which were aluminium. Anyone could see in from the waist up. I looked out. No-one on the veranda and no-one in the playground.

I turned to the still silent class of fifty-six grade ones, some brown, some white, some mixed. I couldn't see Anselm for a minute. Then I looked to where he usually sat and his head appeared, grinning from between the desks. <u>*He could get from one side of the room to the other and grab something even while I was facing the class.*</u> *I opened my mouth to tell him to sit down and then shut it. I sat down myself. I looked at the three-foot long, four-inch wide blackboard ruler and laid it across the desk. My hands were still shaking but my breathing was slowing down. I looked out at the class and started seeing individual faces. If I caught their eyes they looked down. The four overhead ceiling fans continued to whiz and purr. I began to feel the warm breeze from the one near my table. Most of the kids had picked up a crayon or a pencil by now and were looking back to their reading readiness books. Fifty-five witnesses to me belting a little kid, an aboriginal kid. I looked over to where Anselm was aiming his ruler with the paper-wad ammo at his mate. I stood up, walked over to him and took the ruler and the saliva-wet paper and dropped them into the bin. How long to recess?*

Probably because I wanted to spend more time with Anselm himself, I asked her to open out the sentence, "He could get from one side of the room to the other and grab something even while I was facing the class." She wrote:

What the heck? Squealing coming from the back of the room where I'd sent four of the girls to get the tins of pencils sorted while we were chanting at flashcards on the mat.

"I get it Miss," Joy was up on her feet and heading for the noise. She bumped into the first desk. "Owww," twirling around on one leg.

"Get away, get off me," Ann was shrinking into the corner and holding her arms up to ward off trouble.

"Sit down, all of you," I stood up and handed the flashcards to Bradley, who was right by me.

"Hold these up, Bradley, one at a time, until everybody says it, please." Bradley took the cards and sat down with them, resting them on his lap and holding up the first one. He didn't get a lot of attention from some of the grinning faces on the mat, who were whispering,

"That humbug he did it."

"Naw, not 'im, you did it."

"Not me, did not."

At the back of the room Janet started crying. She bent over and was huddling into Mary, who was patting her on the back and looking for me. As I got to them I called back,

"I can't hear any flashcards."

"Phillip's got them Mrs Earle, and he won't give them back," Bradley said. Ye gods. I reached Janet and put my arm around her and turned back to the class. A long stare from me and Phillip handed back the cards to Bradley in a jumbled pile.

"What is it, Janet?"

"He threw it at me, Mrs Earle, and I don't like them."

I looked down to see what she meant just as Joy stamped down hard with her thong. When she lifted her foot we could see the little gecko in its death throes. Janet snuffled and hiccupped.

"That Anselm bugger," Joy said, bending down to pick up the lizard and marching it off in the direction of the bin.

"You can run and put it in the garden, Joy." Bless her. I turned back to the girls and said, "Mary, will you take Janet to wash her face and get a drink of water please?"

"Yes, Mrs Earle."

The class watched them go out and me walk down to the blackboard where I picked up the big ruler.

"Where's Anselm?" Fifty hands gave him up.

"Where's Anselm?" indeed. He has become an even more wily shape-shifter, the invisible scourge of the classroom. Instead, we've been given all the other characters – Janet, Joy and Bradley, and most importantly, the I-character. Freed from her preoccupation with her own guilt, which dominated the first piece, she's now one of a number of players, all of whom have a role to play in moving the action forward. The I-character is coalescing as the one who fusses and fumes over her charges, who in turn have become more complex and less united. Yes, she may be nearing the end of her rope, but she means well. Whereas in the earlier piece, I was so closely identified with her viewpoint that all I could see was the homemade dress that billowed out as she whipped the child, now I can see her whole. And that's because the author has a much better grasp on her too.

~

Understanding the characters who walk through your pages is a vital step toward writing powerful stories. Your understanding will inform those characters and allow them their freedom on the page – leaving you free to experience the sense of discovery (and sometimes even amazement) that is surely one of the great joys of writing. Throughout your writing life, you'll come across people who say they make their characters up consciously, and those who say, in effect, "This stranger just sat down on the end of the bed and started talking to me." You'll also meet writers who say they take the impetus for their characters from life. No one method is better than any other, in my view, as long as you find a way to inhabit those characters consciously and thoroughly, so that you get to know them both inside and out.

Writing Experience

FREEFALL WRITING: CONSCIOUS CHARACTER

1. Turn to a character in your previously-written Freefall who you don't understand very well. Choose a particular sentence that refers to one of their actions, and "open it out" in the way I have described in this chapter. See if, having done so, you feel you know them better.

2. Go back to some earlier Freefall and throw a new experience in the path of the point-of-view character. What can you infer about that character from how they dealt with this new experience?

3. Take some of the Freefall you're interested in from the past, and look to see if your main character takes an active role. If not, decide what it is she or he deeply wants, and would strive to achieve. Freefall a scene or two of that active striving.

4. Choose a character from your Freefall Writing who you really don't like, and give him or her one of your mental habits. Freefall a scene with that character.

5. Make a list of undesirable obsessions. Now, pick (or include) an obsession you have experienced and freefall your way into a scene in which you were in its grip. Next, using your list, choose an obsession you've never experienced, and freefall a scene in the grip of that one, using the emotional truths of your previous scene.

6. Have you ever:
   a) Betrayed someone?
   b) Physically hurt someone on purpose?
   c) Stolen something?
   d) Cheated at something?

Freefall those scenes. You're on your way to understanding "the baddies".

47

Writing Tip: If you find yourself thinking too much in any of these exercises, go directly to a scene, and write it. Remember to write what comes up for you, give all the sensuous detail, don't change anything, and go fearward. And tell the internal critic to stay out of the way. As a friend of mine likes to say, "If it's worth doing, it's worth doing badly".

TIMED WRITING: OPENING OUT CHARACTER

Choose some pieces of Freefall Writing that have characters you'd like to spend time with, and have your writing partner look through them for specific points at which he or she needs to know more. If you're writing on your own, look for places where those characters' motives are obscure or their behaviour seems strange to you.

Open out several of those places for 15 minutes each and see what you come up with.

Writing Tip: Don't explain or analyse anything in these passages. Just open up that specific event in more detail, or write another scene that comes up for you with regard to the same sort of behaviour.

Chapter Six
Discovering Plot

A n awareness of the essence of what you want to write, as we've seen, brings into focus what you want from your novel or story: the question you want it to answer or, as I prefer to think of it while I'm writing, the field in which you want to play. Now that you've begun to form some intimacy with the players – your characters – and, if they're based on real people, to extricate them from the situations in which you've known them, you've taken the first steps toward discovering the plot: the actions and interactions these characters will engage in.

You already know how to follow what has energy for you as you write, to stay with it and see where it takes you. And you've also learned to show (as opposed to simply recounting) the events that arise for a character (often a past self) in connection with that energy. Now is the time to see what has energy for the characters you've currently chosen to engage with: what they want, and what incidents arise for them in connection with that wanting.

At the end of *Writing Without a Parachute*, I quoted Australian novelist Rosemary Stevens' description of how the Freefall process works for her in writing fiction. I think it's well worth taking another look at that in the context of plot:

Before, when I would freefall, the writing would keep looping out and out, until sometimes, I'd lose the thread. Not always. But it always seemed so rich and productive. This, I think, is exactly as it should be with freefall in the beginning – just following the scent and seeing where it leads. And it may go all over the place. But, with the chapters – with a piece that's coming together in a novel – I can now see how you can freefall totally – but it's a different knack. You have one foot in the camp of knowing more or less where you're going and who the characters are, etc, and one foot in the "not knowing" camp, where you just freefall into it. Basically, I'm learning to just place myself in a scene and leap off. This is thrilling because I can see the ground coming up and the parachute does get me there without crashing. (I think I was concerned before that it would waft me out to sea, which wasn't, necessarily, the safest place to land.)

As Stevens points out, when you're writing a novel, you'll already know some things, such as who your characters are and what they're like, what world they inhabit, and the essence of what you want your book to be about. Perhaps you'll even know "where you're going": you'll be aware of some particular events you want to include, or a major event you're heading towards. But within that context, once again you're freefalling what happens in each scene. Writing is not the same as thinking, and it's writing that will reveal to you what no amount of forethought can plan.

Proceeding From Scene to Scene

As you'll already be aware from having written a considerable amount of Freefall, once you begin "showing" rather than simply "telling" something – when you proceed moment by moment, with dialogue and specific sensuous detail – the writing falls naturally into scenes. These days, most novels, many memoirs, and virtually all short stories proceed from scene to scene. Half-scenes and summaries have their uses, which I will be discussing in Chapter Seven. But staying in the kind of intimacy with your characters that "showing" demands – close up, one step at a time – is what will help you to discover their plot. This close to them, there is very little room for thinking, or even remembering. You "just say" and in the creativity of that moment, the actions of the story arise.

If you find yourself stalled or stuck with regard to what comes next, take a look to see if you've backed off into "telling". If you stay close to your characters and to their desires, they will show you what they need to do. All you need to do is keep providing the obstacles – other characters, perhaps, whose desires conflict with theirs – and these too will occur to you as you write.

One caveat: although I am not an advocate of purposely mulling over your story when you're not actually writing it, I do recommend paying close attention to what arises unbidden. I find the moments when I first wake up unusually rich in insight, as if knowing is free to arise from somewhere beyond my personality at such times. And I can vividly remember one occasion when, feeling rather stuck as to how to go forward in the novel I was writing, I decided to stop writing for the day. But as I turned my head away from the writing, already thinking about what I was going to do next, I caught the whole of the next scene as it flashed through the back of my mind. If I had just got up from the desk without pausing, I would have missed it altogether. Writing seems to function almost like dreams do. Sometimes you have to catch it on the fly.

To Plan or not to Plan?

As you begin to find out what your characters will do in one scene after another, the sense of unknowing, which is the flip side of this whole adventure, may start you asking, "Shouldn't I be planning this? Shouldn't I know in advance what the plot will be?" Certainly, there are many writers who do. Strong advocates of outlines, flash cards, or an iron-clad premise, they espouse – often fairly stridently – what works for them. But what I have discovered is that there are at least as many writers who advocate with enthusiasm the method of just finding out what happens as they go along.

When I began to write fiction, I signed up for a programme which required that I send sections of the novel I was writing to an experienced mentor. Mine was novelist Timothy Findley. One of the other requirements of the programme was that I provide an outline of the novel I intended to write, so I duly wrote one. The first communication I received from him was an adamant warning not even to consider following any sort of premeditated outline: "Working to a format is death!,"[11] he wrote, with characteristic theatrical intensity. So I tossed out the outline, glad to be released from the burden of attempting to make the novel adhere to it. What followed was a wild ride – sometimes scary, sometimes glorious – in which I discovered each day where the novel would take me.

Not long afterwards, I was delighted to come across an interview with American writer and humourist, James Thurber. In it, he recounts a situation that arose between him and a co-writer:

I don't bother with charts and so forth. Elliot Nugent, on the other hand, was a careful constructor. When we were working on The Male Animal *together, he was constantly concerned with plotting the play. He could plot the thing from back to front – what was going to happen where, what sort of a situation would end the first act curtain, and so forth. I can't work that way.*

Nugent would say: "Well Thurber, we've got our problem, we've got all these people in the living room. Now what are we going to do with them?" I'd say that I didn't know and couldn't tell him until I'd sat down at the typewriter and found out. I don't believe the writer should know too much where he's going.[12]

I found that many other writers had gone on record as saying much the same thing. They might have some general idea of what they wanted to have happen: a list of events they want to include, or a particular event they want to work toward (as Forster says he did, with the Malabar Caves[13]). But after that, it's a process of discovery. "I've always figured the only way I could finish a book and get a plot was just to keep making it longer and longer until something happens... you know, until it finds its own plot" (Nelson Algren);[14] "Generally I don't even have a plot. What happens is that my characters engage in an action, and out of that action little bits of plot sometimes adhere to the narrative" (Norman Mailer);[15] "I work away a chapter at a time, finding my way as I go" (Aldous Huxley).[16]

Since for most people who have been drawn to Freefall in the first place, one of the most engaging features of writing *is* the element of discovery, doing little or no pre-planning tends to be the most compelling way to proceed. As long as you keep checking in with your original notion of the essence of what you're doing, what it is you want to explore, the events that do arise will have some coherence. Despite the lurking sense of all the time that could be saved by doing otherwise, you work your way, day by day, into the plot of your story. You *don't* know, and then you find out what you *do* know.

Two Shapes of Plot

The chances are that once you have discovered the events that constitute your novel, you'll be able to see in retrospect that it has taken one of the two basic shapes that the plots of most novels seem instinctively to fall into. Either one scene will have succeeded another in a steady course, with each incident proving of more or less equal importance until one conclusive event ends it, or you'll have built a series of events that lead up to a climax which changes everything – followed, often, by some sort of resolution or aftermath.

1. *Episodic*

If your novel has taken the first shape, called "episodic" because of the way one episode follows another, you're not alone. It seems that in every culture where the novel takes hold, this strong shape quickly asserts itself. I think of *Tom Jones* and *Moll Flanders*: no different in plot shape, essentially, from the vast array of thrillers and quest novels that populate our bookshop shelves today. Tom Jones is looking for his real father, and that search takes him through one adventure after another, in much the same way as, say, Henning Mankell's Detective Wallander makes his way through one murder after another, searching for the serial killer. There's a final "aha" of discovery – omigosh, *he's* the killer/father – and then it's finished. The shape is like that of a string of beads, each of which may be intricate in itself but all of which are of equal value, until it closes with a sturdy clasp at the end.

Another way to describe this kind of plot is to say that although the circumstances keep changing, the main character does not. The irrepressible Tom Jones keeps bobbing along on his quest, and all kinds of exciting things happen to him along the way. A change of character for him is never in question – indeed, it's his ability to remain the same that is one of the novel's most charming features. Moll Flanders, having initially been sentenced to death for stealing, ends up in America as a wealthy landowner by using exactly the same skill-set that landed her in Newgate Prison in the first place. She's as invincible and cunning as she ever was, with a buoyant sense of adventure that never flags. We wouldn't have her otherwise, just as we never want the detectives we are fond of to change.

If your plot is turning out to be episodic, you will find it helpful to have an active main character – preferably one who wants something very badly and is prepared to go to some lengths to get it. You may not feel especially drawn by active characters. It only stands to reason that, as writer Janet Burroway notes,[17] many writers may much prefer to spend time with fairly quiet, observant, and possibly rather passive characters like themselves.

But in a novel, things need to happen on the page: we need action, in addition to thinking and talking or even remembering. I was interested to see Janet Fitch, author of the classically episodic novel, *White Oleander*, make the observation that her book became much easier to write when first the I-character's mother, and then the I-character herself, developed into strong-willed characters. Her conclusion is that for the writer,

> [...] *strength of will in a character is the most important thing. If the character has strength of will, you're on the train and they are the locomotive. If your character doesn't know what they want, and they're sort of drifting around then you're pulling the train yourself, which is a lot more work.*[18]

That metaphor seems a very apt way to put it.

People often ask me whether a mystery story or thriller has to be plotted in advance, given that such books often depend on a plot that is a linked chain of events, and are well known to be among the most "plot-driven" novels of all. I can only point out that once again, opinion on that subject among crime-writers seems to be divided. Yes, many do pre-plot their novels carefully. But just as with writers of any other genre, there are those who find it more exciting to find out what happens as they go along. "I just get my characters together and let them interact for a couple of hundred pages," Canadian mystery-writer, L. R. Wright, once told me in an interview, "That's how I find out who they are and what they want." Then she laughed and added, "I don't find out who did it until you do." Crime novelist Elmore Leonard has said much the same.[19]

2. Wedge-Shaped

If the shape your plot takes is that of a slow build-up of events, leading to some ultimate climax, you're also in good company. I call this wedge-shaped plot "Aristotelean", because it was he who first took note of (and prescribed) it with regard to Greek tragedies, in the *Poetics*. It's another shape that's deeply instinctive to the human psyche: not only is it the rhythm of the sex act, it's also the rhythm of every sort of human emotional catharsis. Tension mounts to a climax, whereupon there is a natural release, often accompanied by a change of state or perspective. Probably because this shape is so instinctive, the novel quickly took it up (think Richardson's *Pamela*), and it has been a standard feature of "character-driven" novels ever since.

As with the episodic plot shape, here too the main character or characters want something, but have to contend with the obstacles that stand in the way of fulfilment. But in this sort of plot, with each conflict the problem becomes more difficult or complex, until things come to a head. At that point, the climax, some greater insight may become possible, for the character or for the reader, or both.

Aristotle called this moment of reversal *peripeteia*, which he defines as "a [sudden] change [over] what is being done to the opposite [...] according to likelihood or necessity",[20] often conjoined with recognition (*anagnorisis*), which he defines as "a change from not-knowing to knowing".[21] A clear example of this kind of reversal for me is the story of David and Bathsheba in the Old Testament. David appears to be a man who has everything. He's the king, he has many wives, and he's been steadily victorious in battle. But no. He sees Bathsheba from a rooftop while she's bathing, and he wants her very badly. Her husband Uriah is away at battle, so he sleeps with her and she becomes pregnant. When Uriah returns, David tries to get him to sleep with Bathsheba, but as a soldier in the midst of battle, he refuses. So David instructs his commander, "Put him in the forefront of battle and then withdraw from him, so he may be killed." When the messenger returns from battle, David asks him how it's going. Not so well, says the servant, we lost this, and this and this. But (the commander has told him to save this for the last), "Thy servant Uriah was killed also." So David, overjoyed, takes Bathsheba for his wife. Surely, his plan has been a complete success.

But at this point in the story, a wholly new perspective arises with the narrator's pronouncement, "But the thing that David had done displeased the Lord." He has forgotten that there is another whole level of reckoning. Now all he has achieved has turned to ashes, because he forgot one vital thing about how the world works. It's a classic moment of reversal and recognition.

Fortunately for writers who find the events of their novel gathering to an ultimate climax, there's no real need to worry about *peripeteia* and *anagnorisis*. Insight and recognition, knowledge and self-knowledge seem to be the natural offspring of crisis and the release of tension that crisis can provide. What I'm describing here is what typically happens, rather than what must happen. And that's an important distinction to bear in mind.

Characteristics of this wedge-shaped plot have also found their way into the short story – especially, it could be argued, the experience of *peripeteia*. A short-story tradition that was hugely popular well into the 20th century was the final "twist" or trick ending, a device impressed on the popular psyche by writers like O. Henry and De Maupassant.

In this sort of short story, the main character's obsession takes the reader into an increasingly narrow field of choices, until the author opens it up again with a final twist. In De Maupassant's well-known story, "The Diamond Necklace", for example, the main character, driven by the desire to advance her social status, borrows a diamond necklace to wear at the opera where, alas, she loses it. She buys a similar one to return to the owner, and spends the rest of her life doing manual labour to pay off that debt. Old and coarsened, she runs into the diamonds' owner on the very day she finishes repaying it, and victoriously tells her about what really happened. Her life has been hard, but at least she has managed to salvage her pride. But then comes the twist. "Oh! my poor Mathilda!," the necklace-owner exclaims, "Mine were false. They were not worth over five hundred francs!"[22]

To me, there's a clear connection between this kind of ending and the "sudden change over what is being done to the opposite", "according to likelihood", of *peripeteia*. Yes, that possibility was always there. But we so identified with the main character's obsession that we missed it. We disappeared down a funnel with her, and when we came out at the other end again, we could only stand there blinking in the light.

Nowadays the popularity of the "twist" ending has waned, but an echo of it survives. Often, in a short story, there comes a point of which you can say, "After that, nothing was the same." For a short-story genius like Anton Chekhov or Raymond Carver, that moment may be almost imperceptible, the impact of the first pebble of what could become an avalanche. Part of Alice Munro's genius is to make such moments occur offstage, or only in the mind of the reader. Without such a moment somewhere on the horizon, a short story can feel oddly pointless or flat.

The same echo can be felt in the shape of an individual scene (in a novel or a story). If you have a scene in which someone wants something, overcomes some obstacle, and gets that thing, it all feels a bit pat. Why would you want to read on? But if that character wants, struggles, gets that thing, and then it turns out not to be what they thought it would be – if, in other words, there's a bit of a twist to the ending or a sting in the tail – that scene is going to draw you forward, the character's desire still strangely unfulfilled.

To describe these traditional plot-shapes and some of the effects they typically achieve is not, of course, to say that you need to try to create one when you're writing fiction. The fact is that your plot may well take one of these shapes, or some combination of both, quite instinctively, as it emerges. You may also find yourself instinctively working against these shapes. It's safe to say that on some level, we've all been aware of them, ever since we started listening to fairy tales. My own preference is for such awareness to be conscious, since as Jung pointed out, "Until you make the unconscious conscious, it will direct your life and you will call it fate."[23]

Writing Experience

FREEFALL WRITING: WHAT NEXT?

Choose a piece of Freefall Writing in which events occur on a particular day. Now freefall what happens on the next day. And on the day after that. Do this with three different Freefall pieces, and see if in one of them, the tension can build rather than dispersing.

Writing Tip: When I'm stuck about where to go next with a story, I find walking extraordinarily helpful. I think of this as "walking the plot". If I can let my mind float, and not think about anything in particular, the next scene will often well up unbidden. *Solvitur ambulando*: it is solved by walking.

TIMED WRITING: CONTINUITY

Write a) and b) as separate ten-minute exercises, using the same situation. While you're writing a) try not to think about b) at all.

1.

   a) No way out
   b) Finding a way out

2.

   a) Making the best of a bad situation
   b) Finding a better way

3.

   a) An unsolved mystery
   b) A solution

4.

   a) All I wanted was…
   b) Getting what I wanted

Now, go back and see whether you could have allowed for the possibility of b) in a).

Writing Tip: (This is actually a reading tip.) Read some classic short stories twice ("The Diamond Necklace" by Guy de Maupassant; "Miss Brill" by Katherine Mansfield; "A Good Man is Hard to Find" by Flannery O'Connor; "A Small Good Thing" by Raymond Carver). Can you see how the possibility of the outcome was allowed for by the narrator, early on?

Chapter Seven
Devices

Writing the first draft of a novel, I find it useful and important to move from scene to scene. Coming in this close with the characters, I find out what they love and how they love. I discover what they want and what they're willing to do to obtain it. I learn what obstacles stand in their way. It's as if I need to open everything up as far as possible to place *myself* fully inside the action, so that I can feel it happening all around me and discover what comes next.

One of the great strengths of Freefall Writing is its ability to lead writers so fully into the moment of the scene being written that they no longer feel as if they are wholly controlling the writing. The world of the story, the characters in it, and the story itself are having their say. When a writer has spent enough time in that particular crucible, there's very little desire left to evade emotional complexity, or to fail to come as close to the action as the story requires. And that degree of sustained absorption (not to mention surprise) in the writing begets a desire for more. Most of us wouldn't have it any other way.

But once the plot of the novel has been revealed and the characters realised – once, in other words, you've used this way of engaging with the scenes that arise to discover your story – you may find, on looking back at it, that the story needs to move faster. Not everything needs to be shown. But what other choices do you have? You may also have found that not everything *can* be shown. Background information needs to be imparted. But how do you step outside the action to bring that about?

In this chapter, I'd like to talk about some of the choices you do have: devices you can use to condense the action, or to provide background, while at the same time maintaining the life-like flow of your story.

The Summary

By the time you have fully explored the scenes of your novel or short story, it will probably be self-evident which ones are vital to the story and need to be shown in full, and which can be abridged to keep the story moving or the tension strong. You may also be aware of stretches of time in the characters' lives that you need to pass through quickly as you move from one significant moment to another in the story's span. In situations like these, the summary – something you've learned to avoid as "telling" while the story was coming into being – becomes a useful tool.

Gone are the days when an "intrusive author" could step in and speed things along by addressing the reader directly. Nowadays, the pressure is on to preserve the life-like spell of the story, the "vivid and continuous dream"[24] of it, without interruption. In the service of preserving that spell, the author's need to summarise or "tell" is often either attributed to the character, or disguised as "showing".

How you choose to handle a summary depends partly on which point of view (first, second or third person) you are using to tell the story. When the story is being told in the first person ("I"), the summary can be treated in much the same way as the intrusive author used to treat it in centuries gone by. The first-person character who is narrating can simply announce that need to summarise as their own:

There is almost no point in talking about the rest of the evening, such is its dismal predictability. Stephen flatters me. I feel desired and stimulated. I see, as if for the first time, how unhappy my relationship with David makes me, and I go home wanting out. Oh, and when I get home, David is there waiting, and everything changes again.
(Nick Hornby, How To Be Good[25])

I'll skip all the flying stuff (because recounting it exhausts me almost as much as living it did) and keep this story about the things that happened to us on earth. Basically, it was a nightmare with Ximena Molina (Button)

Miep. Vomit. Wailing. Flailing. Streams of shit. Screams of anguish. Aggie and I were both covered in puke and a little crazy with mortification. Eventually I gave up trying to comfort Ximena and focused on comforting myself with the knowledge that X., my newest baby sister, even with her unfinished features and ruinous needs, was a very honest person. So far.
(Miriam Toews, *Irma Voth*[26])

Even as they purport to show us what the I-character is thinking and feeling, passages like these perform the useful task of summing up a stretch of time in which nothing particularly significant happens.

In first-person novels where the illusion of the I-character's speaking voice is not a prominent feature, summaries are often disguised instead by the use of specific sensuous details, which also serve to make the passage feel "shown" even though a large span of time is being covered. Have a look at this summary, in a first-person novel by Helena McEwen:

What has happened in that time, from spring to autumn, the lifetime of a leaf? What happened when it poked its way through the four small doors, and unfurled its pale-green folded-up pleats to the world? James died. And what happened as the yellow green darkened to summer green, then began to turn yellow at the edge as late summer crept along the branches? Kitty died.
Now the leaves are falling.[27]

By focusing with minute observation on the process of a leaf, the author is able to give what seems like a close-up, while at the same time summarising some significant events and the passage of a considerable amount of time.

In a third-person novel, it's not as easy to step in and offer up a summary. It's a function that has to be performed by the narrator (who stands outside the "he", "she", or "they" of the characters) and too much obvious manipulation by that omniscient narrator tends to weaken a reader's identification with the characters. Here too, a common technique is to disguise the summary with specific detail, so that even as readers are being "told", they feel "shown". In this summary by Joanna Trollope, "small things" not worthy of larger scenes are illustrated with memorable specifics; meanwhile, an entire year is allowed to pass:

Small things happened. Martin was made a junior partner. Natasha started at a little private school in Salisbury – the children wore checked smocks and had to shake hands, smiling, with their teacher each morning – they built on a playroom and another bedroom at the cottage. In late winter, Alice and Martin went skiing (Alice discovered, rather to her satisfaction, that she liked frightening herself), and in the summer, Cecily rented a cottage for them on the north Cornish coast where the children could play in the calm sands of the Camel Estuary. Alice began to read hungrily, novel after novel, carrying lists of them around in her bags along with the purse and cheque books and cash cards and paper handkerchiefs and tubes of Smarties and clean knickers and sticking plasters that formed her daily battle gear. Titles like And Quiet Flows the Don *stuck in her mind like burrs. She chanted them to herself in the car, while in the back the members of the school run bullied the most tearful, sucked their thumbs and surreptitiously took their knickers off in order to amaze the others with their wicked daring.*
(A Village Affair)[28]

A summary like this preserves the illusion of showing the day-to-day world of the characters, even as it gets the job done of moving the story along.

The Half-Scene

Another convenient device for speeding up the story is the half-scene, useful for conveying action which is of no particular significance, but which nonetheless cannot be left out. The half-scene provides another way to sum up while appearing to stay specific – to "tell" while appearing to "show".

This device typically begins with a summary and then, as the name suggests, illustrates it with a short, specific incident from what's being summarised:

The K.L.M. plane was due to take off at three-thirty in the morning for Amsterdam by way of Montreal. Wormold had no desire to travel by Kingston, where Hawthorne might have instructions to meet him. The office had been closed with a final cable and Rudy and his suitcases were routed to Jamaica. The code-books were burnt with the help of the celluloid sheets. Beatrice was to go with Rudy. Lopez was left in charge of the vacuum cleaners. All the personal possessions he valued Wormold got into one crate, which he arranged to send by sea. The horse was sold – to Captain Segura.

Beatrice helped him pack. The last object in the crate was the statue of St. Seraphina.

"Milly must be very unhappy," Beatrice said.

"She's wonderfully resigned. She says like Sir Humphrey Gilbert that God is just as close to her in England as in Cuba."

"It wasn't quite what Gilbert said."

There was a pile of unsecret rubbish to be burnt.

Beatrice said, "What a lot of photographs you had tucked away – of her."

"I used to feel it was like killing someone to tear up a photograph. Of course I know now that it's quite different."

"What's this red box?"

"She gave me some cufflinks once. They were stolen, but I kept the box. I don't know why. In a way I'm glad to see all this stuff go."

"The end of a life."

"Of two lives."

"What's this?"

"An old programme."

"Not so old. The Tropicana. May I keep it?"

"You are too young to keep things," Wormold said. "They accumulate too much. Soon you find you have nowhere left to live among the junk-boxes."

"I'll risk it. That was a wonderful evening."

(Graham Greene, *Our Man in Havana*)[29]

With this brief but poignant exchange between Wormold and Beatrice, Greene can alleviate the potential tedium of getting his character packed to leave the country through the use of a half-scene. In this way, what Virginia Woolf called "this appalling narrative business of the realist: getting on from lunch to dinner"[30] is conducted with aplomb.

Ironically, not long before she denounced "this appalling business", Woolf herself had penned one of the most famous summaries ever written, the "Time Passes" section of *To The Lighthouse*, a "corridor"[31] between two sets of scenes, in which the events of ten years are telescoped by means of a continuing close-up of the family's empty summer-house, with the deaths of major characters conveyed in parentheses. It would be rare for any novelist, realist or otherwise, to accomplish the work of an entire novel without resorting to the useful abridging functions provided by half-scenes and summaries.

Conveying Background Information

Another issue that is bound to arise for any novelist who wants to preserve the illusion of their characters' world intact is one you'll already have encountered in writing Freefall: how to work in the background information you think the reader needs. Now that the narrator's main function is to present events as "shown", the writer often has to resort to one of a number of more or less invisible devices for getting such information across. Here again, the point of view you have chosen (typically first or third person) has a bearing on how such devices can best be used.

First Person Explanation

If you've chosen to write your novel in the first person, then just as you naturally tended to do in Freefall, you can simply have that person tell us what they think we need to know. What they choose to tell us will help to characterise them, even as it provides some useful background information to help the story along.

The way this writer offers background to his scene in Freefall is no different from the method a novelist writing in the first person could use:

I check my watch. Ten minutes to go. Time to stop talking and start writing. I erase all the chipped and pitted chalkboards. I begin on the far left, by the open window where a thick layer of dust has gathered on the sill. It is December, and the Harmattan wind is blowing the Sahara desert into northern Nigeria. It sifts into our shoes; it gets boiled with the rice; it crawls under our fingernails and into our hair; it slips down our necks, mixed with sweat; it gets spat onto the ground when we can no longer stand the taste in our mouths. The dust is everywhere.

"Here's your homework, boys," I say to the class. The students groan and there is a shuffling of notebooks and paper.

"Sir, Abdullahi has stolen my pencil."

I don't take the bait, and keep on writing. "Borrow a pencil, Musa, just like you did yesterday."

Half of the first board is now filled with trigonometry questions. The soft and cheap piece of chalk breaks on a small pothole on the board.

"This is a message from Allah, sir." We all laugh, the boys and me.

I pick up the two useable pieces of chalk from the floor and leave the minor crumbs in the cracks of the concrete. I begin to recite my favourite line from the Koran, and some of the boys join in, having heard me deliver this many times. The ink of the pen of the scholar is more holy than the blood of the martyr.

When I first arrived at the school, the principal begged me to cover the Islamic Religious Knowledge class, promising that it would be no more than one week until he found a replacement for the missing IRK teacher. I had explained that I was not a Muslim.

"Islam is for everyone," the principal said expansively. "I will give you a Koran to read. Just find something that reminds you of a Bible story and use that to teach the boys a moral lesson."

"But I can't read Arabic," I pointed out.

"I can get you an English translation."

I couldn't find polite words to explain to the principal how ridiculous this was. Nigerian Muslims being taught Islamic religious knowledge by the son of a Hindu and the grandson of a Church of Scotland Minister who had so terrified his daughter, my mother, that she converted to Roman Catholicism. He interrupted my thoughts with a ploy he would use often.

"Mister Robert would have done this."

Ah yes. Mister Robert. The Canadian volunteer who had preceded me at this school, GSC Kagara. The super-volunteer who became beloved by the entire town, who learned to pound yam and make bean cakes. The uber-volunteer who left shoes too big to fill, the Canadian volunteer against whom all future Canadian volunteers at GSC Kagara would be measured. And found wanting. Christ, I hated Mister Robert.

(R. Mohan Srivastava)

Just as in a first-person novel, this I-character provides background information in a way that fits smoothly into his story. At precisely the point in the scene when he might imagine a reader would need it (in this case, a reader could be asking, why is someone who is not from this culture quoting from the Koran?), he provides it. So that particular anxiety characterises him: he's someone who feels the need to explain. Perhaps instinctively, this writer has also chosen to convey some of this background information in what is virtually a half-scene, as well – converting what could have been a solid lump of explanation into a species of total recall, the less intrusive and much more lively "flashback".

It's worth noting, too, how much information the writer has worked in – I think of it as "tucked in" – to the first paragraph of this Freefall scene. While he's erasing the blackboard, we're given some vivid sensuous details about the Harmattan: what it is, and how it affects people. This is a good chance to observe that it's a delicate balance. Too much information, and you pull the focus too far away from the scene itself. Too little, and people will be pulled away by wondering what you're talking about. In this instance, the writer has that balance just about exactly right.

Third Person Explanation
When you've chosen to write in the third person, it's tempting to think that you can simply have the narrator step in to deliver the background information you think the reader needs ("Mark had always been a quiet boy, who preferred to read while the other children were playing. This rectitude was due, perhaps, to his mother, who…" etc.). But unlike a first person character's explanations, where our sense of that character's tone of voice and his or her choices is always present, third person background supplied by the narrator does nothing to promote the sense of a character's presence. In fact, it takes away from it. Any attention we pay to the narrator is attention taken away from the characters.

Probably for that very reason, much of what is given by way of background in third person fiction these days tends to arise in a way that could loosely be explained as the character thinking, though nowhere is it directly attributed to them as a thought. What follows is a typical example:

Howard drove home from the hospital. He took the wet, dark streets very fast, then caught himself and slowed down. Until now, his life had gone smoothly and to his satisfaction – college, marriage, another year of college for the advanced degree in business, a junior partnership in an investment firm. Fatherhood. He was happy and, so far, lucky – he knew that.
(Raymond Carver, "A Small, Good Thing")[32]

Rather than a direct thought by Howard, this background information could be said to be *from his perspective*, in a sort of middle ground between the character and the narrator. A phrase like, "so far, lucky – he knew that" almost reflects his tone of voice. Almost, but – since this is the narrator speaking and not the character – not quite.

In most third-person writing these days, there is little or no role for a commenting narrator to play. It's as if, to use a popular image, the camera is sitting right on the point-of-view character's shoulder. It's not inside his head (as it would be if you were writing in the first person) but very close to it. We can see almost nothing that can't be seen by that character, at all (though – and this is where the camera image breaks down – we can also see that character's thoughts).

Whichever person you are using, you can also, of course, have your characters tell each other the background information a reader might need. But be careful not to have that character tell someone something he or she would already know. That's what I call "Superman Syndrome", in memory of the comic books in which Superman so often described some background exploit his readers needed to know about to his hapless assistant, Jimmy Olsen: "You remember, Jimmy, when we stopped Lex Luther from emptying the vault at the Central Bank last week, and he..." Even at eight years old, I would be thinking irritably, "Why are you telling him about this? He was *there!*"

You'll also need to take care not let such an explanation go on too long. Telling is telling, even if it's one of your characters who's doing it.

The Flashback

In contemporary fiction, probably the commonest way of giving background information, in both first and third person, is the flashback: a scene conveyed as if the character is actually re-living the past. The virtue of this device is obvious: information is shown, not told, in a lively and engrossing way. All of us are familiar with how this works in film, where suddenly we are back in an earlier scene – say, from the character's youth – which shows us something vital to our understanding of what's going on in that character's present. In a novel, flashbacks serve the same function of supporting, deepening or otherwise giving background to the main story. Just as in film, they have their virtues and their drawbacks, but in fiction they can be handled in a couple of different ways.

Here, from *Freefall*, is a flashback that begins, more or less spontaneously, in the third paragraph:

I sat on my bed while the others returned to the room. What now? What were we to do? There I was with five girls ranging from form six down to me and Daphne, all shapes and sizes. We would all have to get undressed. How do you do that in public? I wish I had made Mum buy me a nightie rather than pajamas because then you could somehow wriggle out of your top half quickly put the nightie on then pull everything else off or let them fall to the ground without any one seeing.

This was so reminiscent of when mum had said, "You know you are growing breasts. I can see them through your jumper". Oh no she had used that horrible word and worse still she had seen them too. I had noticed "it" happening but thought I could pretend it wasn't or perhaps even prevent it getting worse. Why did she have to bring that up? "I think we'll have to go to Miss Pinkerton's to get a bra." "Couldn't we just go to Marks and Spencer's and buy one?" That was code for couldn't we just dash in when no one else was around and buy one of those horrible things, without speaking to anyone. "No, you need to be fitted and Miss Pinkerton can do that. We will go tomorrow."

I hoped we would get the Young Miss Pinkerton, the smaller, younger, gentler one who usually lingered in the back of the shop winding bias bindings back onto their cards, or straightening the Butterick dress patterns in their boxes. "Nice day Mrs Hannay, and oh how's the young lady?" Damn, we'd got Miss Pinkerton The Older. She turned to me bobbing her head back and forth, followed by a grimace that reminded me of the capuchin monkeys in the zoo. Don't look at her hairy chin. Don't look. "We've come to buy a bra," my mother says far too loudly. Sssh, The Other Miss Pinkerton, lurking in the background might hear. Miss Pinkerton's beady eyes light up, and [she] fixes them on me, "Come with me my dear."
(Alison Lewis-Nicholson)

In the second paragraph, the I-character is reminiscing, remembering snatches of dialogue and commenting on it, but in the third, a flashback begins – a full scene, which proceeds from one moment to the next, with dialogue. (That scene then continues in a very immediate way to its conclusion, whereupon we're restored to the main story with, "So here I was with five other girls and the dilemma of undressing.") All of these memories, but the flashback especially, give background context for the character's sense of modesty and the "dilemma of undressing" in which she now finds herself.

The immediacy of any flashback, however, is also its potential drawback. Here, because the writer is exploring in Freefall, any scene that comes up might open into a potentially new story. But in fiction, the function of the flashback is to support the main story by providing supplementary information. When the scene conveyed in a flashback becomes more engrossing than the main story, it is no longer performing that supportive role. It has taken over.

If you are writing in the first person, the point-of-view character, "I", will experience the flashback. In the third person, you have two choices. You can simply situate the character in the time of the flashback and present it, or you can give the flashback to the character, so that he or she experiences it *as* a flashback.

But whichever point of view you're using, balance is again the important thing. It's up to you decide how long a flashback your main story can sustain before it begins to detract from the main story. This is an especially fine point if you've given the flashback to a character. How long would they really tend to absent themselves from what's going on in the main story, as they remember the past? And is there a reason why this particular memory would come to them at this particular moment? And does the fact that they've just experienced such total recall change them? A flashback which occurs spontaneously within the mind of a character is a psychological event for that character, after all.

~

A last word of advice: before you use any of these devices for giving background, be absolutely sure that this background is needed. Never underestimate the power of a scene to do away with a reader's need for information. Don't forget that your reader is your creative partner and as such – even with very few tips from you regarding what led up to a particular scene – willing to do a large part of the work of filling in the background. "A picture is worth a thousand words" is an old cliché for a reason. Your scene may already be conveying far more information, just by showing your characters in action, than you would ever have imagined it could.

Writing Experience

FREEFALL WRITING: SUMMARIES AND FLASHBACKS

Choose an intense relationship that has a trajectory (a beginning, middle and end) and freefall the scenes that have the most energy for you. Give no background; simply plunge into each of those scenes and write them.

Now, write whatever brief, narrative summaries you need in order to convey what happened in the time that passed between those scenes.

Finally, look back and see if any additional background information is needed. If so, see if you can work it into the scenes as you have written them, without changing very much. If not, try having the point-of-view character furnish that information, either in a few words (as a memory) or as if he or she is experiencing total recall (a flashback).

Writing Tip: Keep a record of the ways you actually remember. In your writing journal, make note of how and why a memory comes up for you, and to what degree you become absorbed in it. (This can become especially obvious in meditation.) Use this information to "naturalise" the way your characters' memories and flashbacks occur.

TIMED WRITING: TELLING AS SHOWING

1. Take three scenes you've written in Freefall and convert them into half-scenes, summarising the action that takes place there, and then giving a conversation or brief incident that typifies that action. (15 minutes each)

2. Take the narrative summaries you created in the "Freefall Writing" exercise above and convert them into half-scenes, in the

same way: a summary followed by a brief, "shown" example. See if any of the dialogue you used in the original scene can be used in the half-scene; if not, create something new that can typify what took place there. (20 minutes each)

3. Take a third-person scene from your Freefall and give the point-of-view character a flashback within that scene. Now do the same, but let the narrator give the flashback.

Writing Tip: Beware of the "hall of mirrors" effect created when a character who is experiencing a flashback recalls something that happened even earlier, creating a flashback within a flashback. One at a time is enough.

Chapter Eight
Dialogue in Fiction

With very little prompting, virtually everyone who writes Freefall learns to let their characters speak out loud. Direct speech is easy and fun to write; in fact, it almost writes itself. Characters seem to be delighted to talk to each other, and what they say is often full of surprises for their authors as well.

The value of dialogue in writing is indisputable. It's a lively and immediate way to show what a character is like and what's important to them. With the advent of film and television, the sense that dialogue is a worthy vehicle for carrying the plot has grown by leaps and bounds. And of all forms of showing, dialogue counts as the most convincing. Someone's opinion might, after all, colour almost anything else that is shown to us, especially via first-person narration. But as readers, we accept without question that whatever occurs within inverted commas is *what that speaker said*. If you are writing in the first person, dialogue is just about the only means at your disposal to get away from that first person's voice, and let some air in.

However, when it comes to writing fiction, the exploration provided by simply having your characters talk to each other is not enough. "Talk is easy. *Let* your characters talk, and they *will* talk. But talk is not a fictional experience," as David Madden has pointed out.[33] Like everything else in the world of your fiction, dialogue needs to accomplish something more than it appears to be doing on the surface. What that more can be is the subject of this chapter.

Subtext

In plays, film and television, where dialogue is the only verbal tool a writer has to work with, and the time-span is limited, writers must constantly ask themselves, "What do I want this dialogue to show?" No passage of dialogue exists to perform just one function. It shows the characters' personalities, how they relate to each other, and above all, hints at a deeper dynamic that underlies the rest of the drama – the subtext to what's being spoken on the surface.

> *Davies: You sleep here, do you?*
> *Aston: Yes.*
> *Davies: What, in that?*
> *Aston: Yes.*
> *Davies: Yes, well, you'd be well out of the draught there.*
> *Aston: You don't get much wind.*
> *Davies: You'd be well out of it. It's different when you're kipping out.*
> *Aston: Would be.*
> *Davies: Nothing but wind then.*
>   *(Pause)*
> *Aston: Yes, when the wind gets up it...*
>   *(Pause)*
> *Davies: Yes...*
> *Aston: Mmnn.*
>   *(Pause)*
> *Davies: Gets very draughty.*
> *Aston: Ah.*
> *Davies: I'm very sensitive to it.*
> *Aston: Are you?*
> *Davies: Always have been.*
>   *(Pause)*
> *You've got more rooms, then, have you?*
> (Harold Pinter, *The Caretaker*)[34]

On the surface, Davies, the homeless man, is simply chatting with Aston about the room Aston has taken him to, to get him away from a brawl. But every utterance in the dialogue between these two men hints at the subtext. Common civility dictates that Aston say *something* in response to Davies, but each time he utters even a single word, Davies converts it to use for his own agenda: to get Aston to give him a place to stay. Sensing the dynamic, Aston tries to say little or nothing, but there's no escaping it. The subtext? Aston is saying, *I won't be trapped.* Davies, alternatively bullying, whining, or wheedling, is saying one thing and one thing only: *take care of me.* The game is on, and Davies seems to have a lot more energy for it than Aston does. How it will continue to play out is the subject of the entire drama.

When you're using dialogue in fiction, it's equally important to keep asking yourself (even if only in retrospect), "What are they really saying?" Or in other words: what is the subtext? What does this scene show that advances the essence of what you're writing?

Fortunately, for people who write Freefall, the conversations that come up between characters are often already rife with subtext. Have a look at this dialogue, for example:

"Is that you Dora?" Deidre sounded impatient.

"Yes." I wasn't used to talking on the phone.

"Could you come for tea on Saturday? Wear something nice, not that red corduroy dress."

"Why?"

"It's a celebration."

"A celebration? What for?"

"Oh for goodness sake. Do you want to come or not?"

"Yes of course."

"Come down a bit early. We're dining at seven, so come down at twenty past six."

"All right. Bye Deidre."

And she hung up without saying goodbye.

I went straight to my wardrobe looking for something to wear. My red corduroy dress was my best and I loved it. I just didn't have anything else.

My mother came in.

"What did she want?"

Normally I wouldn't tell her, but I wanted to put the case for a new dress.

"Deidre's invited me to a special dinner at her place, and she wants me to come early, to help her I suppose, and she said...I mean...I really need a new dress."

"You've just got that perfectly good red corduroy dress that you've hardly worn. You're certainly not getting me to waste my money on a new dress just because Deidre's getting engaged."

"What?" I doubled over as if I'd been punched in the stomach. "Deidre. Engaged?"

"Yes, and I don't know why her parents are allowing it, but she's getting engaged to that Brian Cadd. Far too old for her, but I suppose there's money there."

She went off and I slammed my door and sank onto my bed. Deidre getting engaged. To Mr Brian. What about going to Paris when I left school? And she'd said I could go to Jazz Centre 44 with her. Now she was going to become a boring married woman like my mother. I wished I didn't know. Maybe Deidre had planned to tell me herself. An idea struck me, perhaps as her very best friend I would be her bridesmaid. I could just see myself, with a magically new curve in my waist and a sky blue dress with a wreath of forget-me-knots in my hair. That would be exciting.

Deidre was in the dining room. She looked so grown up, her hair in a French roll, lots of black eye make-up, her long slim neck circled by a pearl choker. She looked me up and down, but didn't comment on my dress.

"Hello Dora, come to my room, we need to have a chat."

I felt as if I'd been called to the head nun's room, something cold and bossy about her voice.

In her bedroom she slammed the door. Before I could stop myself I said, "Deidre, you're engaged! Why didn't you tell me before?"

"Oh who told you?" her voice was loud and cross.

"My mother. Are you really getting engaged to Mr Brian?"

"Stop calling him that."

(Gabrielle Daly)

Deirdre is already impatient, even before Dora picks up the phone, and every word she utters reflects that impatience. Though the ostensible subject keeps changing (from dinner to dress to the ultimate subject of her engagement), Deirdre doesn't seem to have a friendly word to say to Dora. Dora in her turn keeps trying to discover what's underneath that: "What celebration?" "What?" (Why is she getting engaged?) "Why didn't you tell me before?" Neither of them is, of course, saying what they really mean, which is: "I want you to go on being my best friend" (Dora) and, "I've outgrown you" (Deirdre). The humour in the piece comes from the fact that the whole time we're reading it, we're aware of the subtext in a way that the I-character, Dora, is not. Deirdre is marrying her boss, and the friendship is over – a fact poignantly signposted by her last line, "Stop calling him that."

The piece has humour, yes, but it also has the vital ingredient for any kind of "talk" between characters to become dialogue: it has subtext.

Dialogue and Information

It doesn't take long for most writers to discover that dialogue can also function as a useful means of conveying information. Rather than have the narrator intervene to explain something (which, as I pointed out in the previous chapter, can weaken the reader's identification with the characters), characters can simply explain it to each other. What might have had to be "told" can thus be "shown".

But when you find yourself using dialogue for this purpose, be careful. The amount of explaining a character can do out loud, and still appear to be engaging in realistic dialogue, is limited. We are all familiar with the inner cringe that comes when a character in a play or film says shamefacedly, "I guess that sounded like a speech" after delivering some long-winded oration to another character. No excuse can be more than a feeble attempt to disguise the fact that it *was* a speech – a large and undigested lump of monologue in the midst of what should have been a conversation. Too much explanation in a novel draws attention to itself for exactly the same reasons.

The other consideration with regard to conveying information in dialogue has to do with the explaining character's interlocutor. How much can a person listen to with enthusiasm and still come across as a credible human being? Who can forget the Platonic dialogues, with Telemachus *et al* begging Socrates to say more, just when a more typical friend or listener might well be wishing he would say rather less. Clearly, there is only one character in these "dialogues" whose voice is of any interest to its author. If all you have one character saying is, "Is that so?", "Why?", and "Tell me more", then as far as creating realistic dialogue is concerned, you have a problem on your hands. To avoid it, be sure that each character has a believable point of view and is using the interaction to advance it.

Dialogue and Conflict

In fact, the whole secret to useful, realistic dialogue, as far as I'm concerned, lies in giving each character a distinct and recognisable point of view. If you have gone so far as to eavesdrop on other people's conversations, as I suggested in *Writing Without a Parachute*, you'll have gathered plenty of evidence for yourself that, contrary to what you might have imagined about conversation, people don't typically address what their interlocutor just said when they respond. Instead, they advance their own agenda, whatever that might be. And they keep on doing that. That's why the moment the dialogue you write doesn't match up – the moment your character does put forward their own thought, rather than addressing the previous speaker's thought – that dialogue immediately begins to sound realistic, and your readers will recognise this. It's the subtext, above all, that's usually generating what's being said, rather than any particular topic under discussion.

That's one reason why I find "The Same Old Argument" one of the best timed writing topics I can give to introduce dialogue. As it *is* an argument, both characters already have different points of view to advance, and because it's the "same old", these are well-worn grooves for each character to fall into. It's highly unlikely that this oft-repeated dispute will really be about whatever has prompted it this time. The real argument is always about something deeper.

For many of these same reasons, the most powerful dialogue in fiction often arises in conflict. And as novelist Jack Hodgins points out, good dialogue often comes from one particular sub-species of conflict, the power struggle – in fact, he suggests writers keep a list of ways people try to get what they want from each other, to help with writing dialogue.[35] (My own approach to writing comes from the opposite direction: if you go "where the energy is" on behalf of your characters in the first place, you won't need to write from a list.) It is certainly worth noting that virtually every line in the exchange quoted above between Aston and Davies constitutes a move in their mutual power struggle.

80

The same could be said for Deirdre and Dora. The theatrics over Deirdre's engagement announcement all amount to a single-minded attempt to establish her own viewpoint, "I've changed", as dominant, while almost everything Dora thinks and says reflects a single, conflicting directive: "Change back". Pick any novel you're currently reading and examine some passages of dialogue. I think you'll find that most of the conflicts you see there constitute a power struggle of some kind.

When you allow the writing to take you to situations that have energy for you, this sort of conflict tends to arise intuitively. But it's important to bring to consciousness the fact that it *is* happening, so that if you find you need to, you can make that choice.

Dad groaned. "You've gotta get me out of here."

My chest felt tight and tears welled up in my eyes. I would have given anything to take him home but I knew he couldn't cope on his own and I couldn't look after him.

"You'll get out of here as soon as you're better," I said, trying to shine a positive light on the situation. "What do your doctors say?"

Dad began pacing around in the shade of the octagonal courtyard. A green shade cloth blocked out most of the sun, but one corner hung loosely, the sun's full intensity burning the courtyard's sole plant – a wilted, browning banana tree. In the centre, grass clung to life at the edge of a square pit of dirty sand. Cigarette butts littered the enclosed courtyard. "What do they know?" Dad growled. "They dope me up so much I feel like a zombie."

"It's just until you get better."

Dad cried out and began breathing harshly. "You don't understand. You don't know how bad it is."

I nodded. I had experienced depression a few years ago but I'd never been this bad. I reset two upturned plastic chairs and sat in one. I watched Dad pace back and forth, his changing facial expressions revealing how busy his mind was. He was driving me mad. I patted the chair next to me. "Come and take a seat."

"All I do is sit down and sleep all day," he groaned. "I'm putting on weight."

"It looks like you've lost a lot," I said, motioning to his drooping clothing.

"It's these bloody meds they've got me on," he said. He sat down in the seat next to me. At the last minute, I noticed how dirty the seat was and I cringed, feeling guilty for not being a better son.

My mind went blank and so we sat in silence for a while. Eventually, I asked, "How are you?"

"How can you ask that? Look where I am."

I sighed. I couldn't talk to him. I never could when I came here. There was something about this place. "Has Melissa come to see you?"

"Nobody ever comes to see me." His hands fidgeted.

I knew this was a lie. I'd spoken to Melissa before I'd come here. She'd been the one who'd convinced me to come and see Dad.

We sat in silence for a long moment. The drag of Dad's negativity, his illness was already draining the life from me. I wanted to go, to escape. But I hadn't been here five minutes.

He got up and began to pace again.

The glass door shimmied open and Stan, carrying a cigarette and lighter, slid through, before the door slammed shut. I sighed internally. I'd brought us out here so we could have some privacy to talk. Stan wasn't helping.

Stan's lips clamped down on the cigarette and he cupped a hand over its tip. He paused and looked from Dad to me and back again. His eyes lightened up. "Ah tol' yer ah'd seen yer before." He pointed to Dad and then to me. "Yer and him. Yer the same. How come there's two a yer?"

My body shook. I wasn't like Dad. I wasn't. I wasn't going to end up like this.

(A.R. Levett)

In this highly authentic-sounding passage of Freefall dialogue, there is clearly a power struggle afoot. Despite the guilt the son is feeling about his father's situation, there's a rebuttal, spoken or silent, in his every response to him: "Get me out of here"/"No"; "I've gained weight"/"You've lost it"; "Nobody comes to see me"/"You're lying", and so on. What the father wants is crystal clear. He wants to get out of there. But the son's agenda is not made clear until the end of the scene, when Stan's comment brings the subtext of his side of the conversation to the surface: "I wasn't like Dad. I wasn't going to end up like this."

Trust in the Power of Dialogue

Like everything that is "shown" in fiction or in memoir, direct speech often conveys a great deal more than you might have believed it would

82

while you were writing it. It may be only when you look back that you'll discover just how much the dialogue you have invented has made self-evident. How much side explanation or commentary you put in around it will of course depend to some extent on style, and on what you want to show about your narrator, if this is a first person story. But you may well find that many of the explanations you have given about how something was said (the adverbs, for instance), the effect of what was said, or the motivation of the speaker in saying it ("'You'll get out of here as soon as you're better' I said, trying to shine a positive light on the situation") have turned out to be more or less redundant.

So when you do come back to a passage of dialogue you've written, try repeating it out loud (which is probably the way you heard it while you were writing), with an eye to eliminating as many of the narrative comments about that dialogue as you can bear to. Good dialogue is often self-explanatory, and anything additional can come across as at best unnecessary and at worst, controlling (as Elmore Leonard put it, "the writer sticking his nose in"[36]). In theatre, the few stage directions that do survive the play's publication are usually swiftly overridden by the director.

Here is a good reminder of the extent to which strong dialogue can stand by itself:

Sheila, do we get off here? he asked.
Ahhh, I'm not sure.
Sheila, do we get off here or not?
Al, I can't tell.
Sheila!
Yup, that was the exit.
The one we just passed?
I think so.
You think or you know.
I think.
No, you don't think. You don't think cuz you don't have a brain in your head.
Al, she said.
What, you don't want the kids to know you're stupid. Kids, he said, turning his head from the road.
Al, you're driving.

Kids, you know how dumb your mother is. I don't want you to be that
dumb which is why you have to finish school.

And with that he'd turn back, jerk the steering wheel so the car was
straight on the road and drive.
(Dolly Reisman)

How Much Dialogue?

Certainly, things have changed since Edith Wharton described dialogue
in fiction as "an effect to be sparingly used" by writers whose "instinct
will be to record only significant passages of their [characters'] talk, in
high relief against the narrative".[37] These days, most writers use dialogue
to allow their characters to accomplish a great deal of what it used to
be the narrator's job to get across. And modern readers have a much
greater tolerance than they used to have for hearing the characters in
fiction, and even in memoir, talk.

But even though the word "sparingly" appears to have been cast aside,
some of Wharton's other words with regard to dialogue – "significant"
and "instinct" – still apply. Dialogue is bound to be most effective
when your characters have something significant to say. And your own
instinct is the best guide you can call upon to tell you when to stop. To
put it another way, your body knows. When you've let the characters go
on too long, or say something too trivial, you can start to feel restless
or ungrounded. But when no-one is speaking and it's time they did,
you can find yourself feeling claustrophobic, as if there's an invisible
wall to be broken through. Somewhere on the continuum between the
voice of your narration and the "talking heads" of unrelieved dialogue
between your characters, you will instinctively find your balance. The
rhythm of that alternation belongs to you.

Writing Experience

FREEFALL WRITING: DIALOGUE AND SUBTEXT

1.

a) Go back to two or three significant passages of dialogue in your Freefall Writing. Check to see if each of the characters has an identifiable point of view. If not, freefall the same conversation with a clear idea of what each character has in mind.

b) Now, consider what they're really saying (the subtext). Freefall a discussion (or argument) in which the subject is different, but the subtext is still the same.

2. If you don't find much direct speech in your Freefall, use the next few days' Freefall Writing sessions to write direct speech – whatever comes up for you. (If you find it hard to get started, give yourself the "Same Old Argument" topic again to kick off the process.)

3. Have a look at two pieces of Freefall Writing in which you don't use much direct speech. Decide for yourself what central concerns those pieces reflect. Now, open out a couple of dialogue passages in each piece that reflect those concerns in some way.

Writing Tip: One of the natural facts about subtext is that the characters who are speaking virtually never mention it aloud, and often aren't even consciously aware of it. Think of it as a secret only you and your reader share.

TIMED WRITING

1. Write ten-minute dialogue passages based on the following topics (but without using those exact words):
    a. The best excuse
    b. Getting caught in a lie
    c. "You're driving me crazy"

2. Write three ten-minute scenes with NO dialogue.
    a. Seen from the window of a train
    b. Outside the café
    c. Bird life

3. Now combine each dialogue from #1 with a scene from #2, simply alternating between the two as you see fit. [with thanks to Mary Holscher, who gave me the inspiration for this exercise]

Writing Tip: Of the many ways to break up dialogue, alcohol, coffee, and (until recently) cigarettes have been among the most popular. See what other ways you break up your own dialogues with people, versus the ways they choose.

Chapter Nine

Drama

One of the primary reasons why Freefall Writing typically turns out to be so compelling to read is the injunction in the fourth precept to "go where the energy is, or 'go fearward'". What has energy for the writer is almost bound to have energy for the reader. Whatever constitutes "fearward" for a writer usually entails a dramatic situation, toward which the story seems naturally to build. There is action, tension, and a strong forward thrust to the narrative. When the "sensuous detail" precept is followed at the same time, there is also a vivid physical context – the setting – which leaves the writer with experiential awareness of the interplay of action and description, and of how to handle that interplay as the story goes along.

But although this kind of spontaneous unfolding has a great deal to teach a writer, some of the choices available for fiction and/or memoir simply don't arise in this way, or don't arise for everyone. In this chapter, therefore, I'd like to discuss some important considerations for enhancing the dramatic power of a work of fiction, be it a short story, novel, or that seldom-used form, the novella. (Most of these considerations will also pertain to memoir.) None of these choices need interfere with the spontaneity of what does arise, but they are valuable possibilities to consider during the revision process. And of course, once you have internalised them, they become part of a panoply of options that do occur to you spontaneously as the writing unfolds.

Structure

As writers of Freefall, we may not even be aware that what we're writing *has* a structure. That's because most of what gets written in Freefall keeps to the so-called "natural" structure in which – except for the odd flashback – one event follows another in chronological sequence. Given that this is the way that real life tends to unfold, this chronological structure draws very little attention to itself. For the writer as well as for the reader, it's a scaffolding that sustains the story more or less invisibly.

But, over time, fiction-writers have evolved a variety of alternatives to that "natural" structure. Considerations which have to do primarily with drama – the need (whether conscious or unconscious) to keep the tension taut and the characters vivid – have impelled new choices, some of which have greatly increased the impact of what happens in the plot.

One thing many writers – and editors – are sharply aware of is the need to hook the reader's attention from the outset, something that the slow accumulation of events over time is unlikely to do. Often a simple tweak to that "natural" structure is all that's needed.

A good example is Beryl Bainbridge's "thoroughly enjoyable horror experience",[38] *Harriet Said*, a novel about two young girls who commit a murder. I suspect that the book originally hewed to a chronological structure, showing the gradual build-up of factors which led to the murder. But at some point the author or editor had the inspiration to move the (previously) penultimate chapter to the beginning of the book. The opening sentences of the book, therefore, are now the ones that take place in the story just *after* the climax:

Harriet said: "No you don't, you keep walking." I wanted to turn round, and look back at the dark house but she tugged at my arm fiercely. We walked over the field hand in hand as if we were little girls.

I didn't know what the time was, how late we might be. I only knew that this once it didn't really matter. Before we reached the road Harriet stopped. I could feel her breath on my face, and over her shoulder, I could see the street lamps shining and the little houses all sleeping. She brought her hand up and I thought she was going to hit me but she only touched my cheek with her fingers. She said, "Don't cry now."

"I don't want to cry now."

"Wait till we get home."
The word home made my heart feel painful, it was so lost a place.[39]

Had the author chosen to stick with the "natural" structure and begin at the story's chronological beginning, the following paragraph would have opened the novel instead:

When I came home for the holiday, Harriet was away with her family in Wales. She had written to explain it was not her fault and that when she came back we would have a lovely time. She said that Mr. Redman had died and that she had spoken to him only a few days previously. He had inquired what she was going to do when she left school. She said she might go on the buses. "Likely you'll get more than your ticket punched," he had replied. It was a nice farewell thing to say. Harriet said we should bow the head at the passing of landmarks.[40]

There is nothing at all wrong with this beginning. It establishes the ages of the two girls nicely, the fact that Harriet may be beginning to sense the limitations that may arise in her future, and that she has taken on the role of interpreter of life in the village for the I-character. It even introduces the shared sense of *sang-froid* that often characterises the humour of children of that age. But there's nothing particularly gripping about it, either. If I had opened the book and read this paragraph first, I might not have read further. Given the way the book did come to be structured, however, I was completely hooked by the time I'd read the first few paragraphs. These girls have just done something that appalls at least one of them – but what? What could possibly have happened to make home seem "so lost a place"?

What Bainbridge has done, by changing the order of these chapters, is to turn the chronological structure of her novel into the structure most short-story writers use, and many novelists turn to at some stage, summarised as an ABDCE structure: Action, Background, Development, Climax, Ending.[41] Only by plunging us into the action first, and then going into its background, does it stray from the "natural" order of the wedge-shaped plot described in Chapter Six. Events still build to a climax over time. By, in effect, "going where the energy is" in the story immediately, the writer engages us in some action (or, as here, its consequence), leaving a powerful desire for background information in its wake.

A mid-twentieth-century American writer, Clifton Fadiman, identified three common structures in fiction:[42] chronological, converging (in which we follow a number of separate sequences which converge at a particular place and time), and vertical (in which we keep making excursions away from present time, perhaps at the whim of memory, as in À la recherche du temps perdu). The Girl on a Train, a contemporary thriller by British writer Paula Hawkins, owes its popularity partly to the author's re-working of the converging structure, as various narrators move back and forth in time until the killer is finally revealed. Elena Ferrante's passionate Neapolitan novels seem almost to be inventing a new kind of structure, as the first-person narrator moves from obsession to obsession – a lost doll, a hand-made pair of shoes – without much apparent regard for chronology at all. But like the structures of most novels, these could also be said to be variations of the chronological: time marches on while the narrators are changing or circling, and the forward-moving flow of events in time is still served, if only in a subterranean way.

Although we can talk about structure in the abstract, I suspect most writers would be hard-put to say whether they choose the structure for their stories, or whether the structure chooses them. The essence of what is being written may seem to demand a particular structure: a convergence of narrators, or the kind of life-review best served by a novel-long backward glance. My own bias is to believe that the best structure is the one that feels most naturally a part of what you have to show. But given that the dramatic power of what you're writing is also a consideration, it's good to stay aware of the options that are in front of you, both as the material first arises, and in the revision process that results in the final draft.

Setting

As you will have experienced countless times by now in Freefall, the third precept, "Give all the sensuous details", is your reminder to stay physically present in whatever world you're writing about. For your readers, those specific, sensuous details perform the same function:

they make it possible for them to participate in the story physically too, as reminders to smell, feel, taste, hear and see what is happening along the way. Anchored in the body, it becomes much more possible to feel the characters' feelings, if you're the writer, and to experience them as your own if you're the reader.

Yet whenever I first introduce that third precept, someone almost inevitably says, "But I don't like a lot of physical details. I find I always skip over those when I read." This makes me realise just how often those details are presented in a separate, "skippable" lump in in the course of a story,[43] rather than as information that emerges naturally along the way. Too often, it's as if we're being asked to take time out from the narrative to take in the description, with the promise that when we've done that, we can come back to it. It's little wonder people resist it, and want to get back to the drama again.

If you follow that third precept, and keep your attention attuned to the physical details of your character's experience *as* you write, the setting will simply be present as part of the action. Take a look at this example from Freefall:

You let me sleep well past the start of my watch. You steered alone, watching the barometer fall, and the waves build. The wind instruments jam in the shrieking gusts. Finally you call me up from my lee cloth cradle down below. I don yellow foul weather gear, boots and gloves. On land no one notices the wind changes, or the trees ratcheting back and forth. Out here on the unsheltered expanse, we're exposed to each blast. Through the gloom I see you beckon, the tiller tucked under your arm. "Come sit here. Let your eyes adjust," you reach out to grab my hand. I'm greeted with a drenching of salt water that fills the cockpit way up over the top of my boots. It's the sounds that scare – the slap of breaking waves against the hull, the knocking, crunching punches. The sounds match the savage rocking and thrusting of our little boat – her shudders, her despair as she buries her railing, her scuppers underwater. "Oh my god. This is terrible," I say, giving up. I can't feel my way through these waves.
(Anna Gersman)

This writer never fails to notice what is around her character, or to have her notice, even in the heat of strong emotional turmoil, what's going on in the physical world she occupies. As a result, we too can feel the setting viscerally, as part of the action. The yellow foul weather gear, the gloom on deck, the "knocking, crunching punches" of the waves: I can't imagine anyone saying they don't want these physical details. They're far too vital to the drama that's taking place.

Another effective way for the setting to make itself felt is to allow it to filter in through inference, while the character's attention is focused elsewhere, so that the setting grows up around him or her, even though it has not been directly mentioned:

At supper Mother said to Father that the kids were terrible. And how could she invite Mrs. Hallman in? He hadn't built the cage he'd promised for a month and Rudy let Jeepers loose again in the kitchen and Sharon wouldn't come down from the kitchen table. She'd offered Mrs. Hallman some tomatoes, but they're allergic to tomatoes, and it was too bad, but she couldn't play bridge with Mrs. Hallman because she had better things to do with her time.

When Mrs. Hallman came for coffee, Mother would send me to the cellar for a jar of jelly and spread a clean tablecloth. Then she would sit drawing circles with her finger, smiling and nodding while Mrs. Hallman rattled her charm bracelet and talked about Toronto and Minneapolis and "my husband the doctor." I would sit listening to her wind-chime laughter, unable to move when told to go out and play with the others.

When Mrs. Hallman left, Mother would bang pots and pans on the stove, or put on Father's fishing hat and chop weeds in the garden, making chunks of earth fly up around her feet.
(Sandra Birdsell, "Stones")[44]

In this short story, which she claims to have written during a timed exercise in a writing class, Birdsell establishes a vivid sense of the atmosphere of this household using almost no direct description. Again we're caught up in the action, so that whatever details come our way remain secondary to our experience of what's taking place there. But in fact they're given largely by implication. If the mother "spread a clean tablecloth" when her guest came, we have to infer that the usual tablecloth was not so clean. We also infer that the kitchen is where they receive guests, that Jeepers (a mouse? a rat?) has been running around the kitchen and that (as a result?) one of the children has been standing on the table. If the father hasn't built the cage he's promised in over a month, we can infer that there may be other things he hasn't done around the house, either, whereas the mother seems to be constantly busy. Mrs. Hallman, with her charm bracelet and her wind-chime laughter, makes the I-character's world leap into focus by contrast, as a chaotic, tumbling disorder, full of children, animals, and the mess of ordinary life. This is a writer who is powerfully embedded in the world she's writing about, physically, yet virtually none of what we can see have we directly been told.

A further important fact about setting, observable in both of the passages I have quoted here, is that active verbs are vital to keeping the physical details present in an active way. Although we're probably all aware that the active voice (the dog bit the boy) is preferable to the passive (the boy was bitten by the dog), what's less well known is that the verb "to be" is essentially passive, too. It's instantly more effective to use an active verb (the chair "sat" or "perched" by the door; "I found a chair by the door") than to use the verb "to be" ("the chair was by the door", or the even more common, "there was a chair by the door"). And the stronger the action, the stronger the verbs can become: "The wind instruments jam in the shrieking gusts" or, "I'm greeted with a drenching of salt water", in the sailing piece quoted earlier. That way, the verbs themselves function as part of the action, even as they work to establish the setting in which that action takes place.

So if you don't want your reader skipping the details of your setting, be sure to keep that third precept in your awareness as you write. That way, almost anything that is important to your character can also become a way of revealing something about the physical world they inhabit. It may help to remember this dictum: *action advances, description retards*. By having your character look around and take things in, by implying more about the physical context than you say, and by using action verbs, you make your setting inseparable from the action: no longer part of the problem, but part of the solution instead.

Person and Point of View

Because confusion sometimes arises as to whether "point of view" refers to person (as in the first, second, or third-person point of view), or perspective (which character's point of view we're going to be identifying with as the story unfolds), I prefer to distinguish between person and point of view, reserving the latter for the character whose eyes we see through and whose thoughts we share. In the first person, this is obviously going to be the "I-character" – the one who says "I". In the second person, the "I" will also be the point-of-view character, even though "you" is being addressed. In the third person, it's a matter of which character or characters the writer chooses to stay closest to – whose shoulder the camera is sitting on as the story unfolds.

Many people who come to writing through Freefall will have already given some thought to the question of which person they choose to write in. When the writing that emerges is autobiographical, some writers try using the third person (he, she) in order to achieve some distance from the material, or to try to disguise its autobiographical nature. If some of that material is later used for fiction, the same issue often arises: should they use the first person or the third?

In the first instance, when you are writing Freefall and autobiographical material does arise, I would strongly advise you to use the first person: just say "I". Using the third person does nothing to disguise the autobiographical nature of the material: it just sounds like someone inexplicably writing autobiography in the third person. And using the third person to distance the material is unnecessary, given the existence of the fifth precept, the "Ten-Year Rule". As a result of that precept, the character you find yourself writing about will be at most a past self, and as such, a character who is no longer you. To try to distance the material further would only hamper your learning one of the important skills Freefall has to offer: the ability to identify closely with the point-of-view character at the same time as you perform all the tasks a narrator must perform.

But when you're writing fiction, whether or not it's in some way inspired by your Freefall, the question of whether to use the first or the third person becomes a valid one to ponder. The first thing to ask yourself if that question comes up is: "How does the story seem to present itself?" Often, the characters simply appear in your mind's eye as seen from the outside (in the third person), or from the inside (in the first person). In this case, the choice has already been made for you – and that above all is the kind of choice I respect. If it feels like a lively option to make that choice deliberately, then it's well worth experimenting until you discover which person is both the best fit for you *and* the most compelling vantage point from which to tell your story.

When the subject of Nigeria first began to emerge for me in Freefall, this scene, for example, emerged in the first person:

At 4 a.m., driving to the village, driving out from town and the party left behind. (I look down at the lights below me, one man said, and I think to myself, I did this. I did all of this. If it weren't for me, none of this would be here.) Driving down the dark highway, snake ribbon of deeper black, I thought, what if my car breaks down, where would I turn? Fringes of thought, fringes of the bush turning orange now in his sodium vapour. Where could I ever go for help? And even as the thought rose, I knew – I could go anywhere. Walk twenty paces into this darkness and there will be welcome, warm mud walls and a fire, hot, thick drinks and soft clicks in the silence. And the murmuring. Hakka ne. Thus it is. Ah-ah. Ba kome.

I could hear them wailing from my bed at night, the man said, smoothing down his tie with one hand, coaxing it back into the fold between his chest and his stomach. Oh, the sound of that wailing. They thought I would let their men out, you see. They thought that kind of thing would work on me.

I have to go now, I said. I have to get going. I tried to say it coldly, to make a point – to make some coward's point that would answer to my own heart for what I could not say. That I was stepping out of that small circle of candlelight and into no-place and no-time and that I loved you. That there was another world entirely, an hour from this living room.

Part of what interested me about pursuing this contrast between worlds into a novel was the fact that the writing was already beginning to move into fiction: while I couldn't actually remember the party where this dialogue took place, I could certainly imagine it. I could see the man and the young woman at the party from the outside, as they spoke. Perhaps that's why, when I did begin to write a novel set in Nigeria, the third person felt like a natural choice. I was sorry to lose the kind of lyric intensity that comes with being inside someone's head, but I could also sense that it could become cloying after a while. When elements of that same scene emerged in the novel in the third person, they had a very different hue:

"I've created this whole grid from ground zero," he said, turning to Sarah again. "There was nothing here at all before I came. Sometimes at night I like to drive up the hill behind Tudun Wada." His voice was becoming softer.

"I look down on the lights of the town and I say to myself, I did this. I did all of this.

"Rural electrification's the thing now," he went on. "One village after another. My goal is to have light in every village on the Plateau before I leave here. Because we'll all have to leave here eventually, won't we, Evans?"

Oh God, Sarah thought. Electricity in the villages? No more darkness? No more silence? Maybe he was right, there would be a war. Maybe they'd throw him out before he got the chance.

"Are you all right?" Sarah saw Mrs. Beresford looking at her curiously and realised she was staring at him.

"Do you know," she said, looking at her watch, "I really should get going. Do you mind, Felix? I've got an early class tomorrow."

Mrs. Beresford rose to her feet as Sarah got up, and smiled her engaging smile. "Will we see you at the Hibernian Ball?"

"Oh, I expect so," Felix spoke up as Sarah started to shake her head. "Can't have too many attractive young ladies."

"I do hope you'll join us. Our party, I mean. You'll let us know, Felix? Hamish is Grand Chieftain again this year."

They all looked at Mr. Beresford, who was biting the top off a fairy cake. "There's some kind of ruckus coming, mark my words," he said, waving to them with his free hand. "I'd be prepared for the worst, if I were you."

When you do try switching person, you'll start to feel their respective strengths and weaknesses almost immediately. "I" is both more gripping and also more limiting: the intensity of the inner can wear thin, and it's harder to move the characters around. To address an invisible "you", as in second person narration, is so limiting that it is very seldom used in fiction, although it has worked successfully in memoir, especially in situations of loss[45]. With the third person, you have to work against a certain distance created by the fact of an outside narrator, but you also have the freedom to use more than one point-of-view character, as long as you give the reader a sizeable chunk of time to identify with each one.

What's important, if you do find yourself deliberating about the choice of person, is to keep checking in with the story and your inner sense of its purpose, sensing which one makes the story feel most alive in you.

Limitation and Centrality

Two other considerations related to point of view that can influence the dramatic impact of your writing are limitation and centrality: how much does your point-of-view character know, and how close to the action are they situated?

Limiting how much your point-of-view character can know or understand about what's going on in the story can exert a powerful torque on the action from a reader's perspective. Think of the terror Stephen King instils into *The Shining*, for instance, by showing that story through the eyes of a child. As adults, we're constantly aware of how much he can't see or understand, which keeps us in an ongoing state of fear for him as we read. Emma Donoghue achieves a similar effect with a child-narrator who has grown up in captivity in *Room*, as do countless other writers who play on the tension between our own inferences and those we see the point-of-view character making. A limited or unreliable point-of-view character can also make for humour for much the same reason (think of *The Curious Incident of the Dog in the Night-Time*, or *The Rosie Project*). From the time of Greek drama, where the chorus so often supplied the information that the protagonist did not know or could not see, writers have been utilising the power of our empathy for a character with a limited point of view.

Freefall writers will often have had some experience using a limited point-of-view character for humour or for drama, simply because so much material tends to arise from childhood. Extending that limited point of view over the length of a whole novel can be tricky (for me, *The Rosie Project* illustrates the problem of having a restricted perspective wear thin over time), but well handled, it can elicit strong empathy and hence involvement in the novel, as it does in *The Shipping News*, for example.

Another question to consider with regard to dramatic impact is how closely the point-of-view character is going to be involved in the action. Sometimes this is simply a given: it's part of who that character is that they jump into whatever is going on, or that they shrink back and observe while other characters hold sway. But sometimes you discover that you do have a choice. And when you do, it helps to bear in mind that the closer the point-of-view character is to the action, the more dramatic the story is likely to be.

At a talk about the first novel in her *Josephine B.* trilogy, American writer Sandra Gulland mentioned that she had first thought of writing a novel about a woman living in a small town (not unlike the one she herself lived in) who was obsessed with Napoleon and Josephine. Then, she said, she had a dream which altered that idea completely. "What was the dream?" I asked. "I dreamt that a group of people had opened a trunk and were trying on eighteenth-century costumes. One couple were dressing up as Napoleon and Josephine. Then they turned and started talking to me, and I realized they *were* Napoleon and Josephine. I woke up knowing I had to write the novel from their point of view, instead." "How did you feel?" I asked her. "I was terrified," she said.

What Gulland did as a result of that dream was to move the point-of-view character, who stood at one remove from the action (obsessing about Napoleon and Josephine's lives), to a much more central position (Josephine is now the point-of-view character, at the heart of the action of the story). For some writers, how close the point-of-view character is to the action is an unconscious decision. For others – as in Gulland's story – it's made semi-consciously, and for yet others, it seems to be deliberate: "I write in scenes and always from the point of view of a particular character – the one whose view best brings the scene to life," says Elmore Leonard[46]. I'm frequently amazed to see how relentlessly playwrights march the character with whom we most empathise right to the heart of the most dramatic situation, the absolute centre of the play.

Of all the arts, only fiction, memoir and poetry steadfastly give us the ability to see the thoughts that the point-of-view character hasn't spoken. Passionate arguments are waged about whose point of view we're entitled to. Can men speak as women, for instance, or white-skinned people as black? These issues arise because point of view *is* such a powerful tool, and the empathy it stimulates is one of our most highly valued traits. Like the structure and setting, point of view has the power to involve us deeply in the drama of another person. So even if our preferred approach to writing is largely spontaneous, it behoves us to be aware of the range of choices that, as writers, we share.

Writing Experience

FREEFALL WRITING: STRUCTURE, PERSON, POINT OF VIEW

1. Take a Freefall story you have written in chronological order, and try altering the structure according to Alice Adams' formula: ABDCE. Next, start near the climax of the same or a different story, and build back up to it in the subsequent scenes. Finally, start with the ending, and build back up to that in the rest of the story.

2. Observe which person you habitually use in Freefall. If it's the first person, try writing from the third, and vice-versa. Try a story in the second person, too. Be aware, as you do so, of the changed demands the use of a different person makes on the story.

3. Choose a piece of Freefall Writing that has two main characters. Experiment in alternating between their points of view (using either the first or the third person for both of them). (Even though a short story is typically too brief to accommodate more than one point of view, it's interesting to play with this as an exercise.)

Writing Tip: If you're using more than one point-of-view character, don't try to make their points of view "match up" any more than you would with dialogue. Situate yourself firmly within the perspective of that character, and you'll find they have their own preoccupations to deal with, entirely different from those of the other character, even if they're dealing with exactly the same situation.

TIMED WRITING: SETTING AND POINT OF VIEW

Write the following as 12-minute exercises:

1. Keep yourself attuned to the "sensuous details" surrounding the point-of-view character as you write on these topics:
   a. Turn and face the strange
   b. The first day of school

c. Were we the first to make love in a...
d. Did my mother? (Something you did)

2. A sound heard in childhood (addressed to the second person: "you")

3. These topics require a switch in point of view:
   a. The best teacher I ever had
   b. My most memorable student (from the point of view of the same teacher you wrote about in "a", bearing in mind the Writing Tip above)
   a. He's fooling himself
   b. No, she is
   a. Write about a crime from the victim's point of view
   b. Write about the same crime from the viewpoint of the perpetrator

Writing Tip: If you're accustomed to writing autobiographical Freefall, don't expect writing from someone else's point of view to feel good at first. What Freefall writers frequently forget is that writing autobiographical Freefall also felt embarrassing at first, because the I-character's perspective was so different from the one they have now. Give yourself time to grow into this new character's point of view.

Chapter Ten
The Genre of Memoir

A nother set of choices we inherit has to do with the conventions attached to each particular genre of writing. If I decide to write a novel, for example, it's good to know what expectations have coalesced around that form. If I say I'm writing a short story, what do other people understand that to imply? Does the fact that I'm writing a memoir mean that everything I write there is expected to be true?

Of course, it may well be that what I write will flout my readers' expectations of that form. Like everything else, our writing has meaning within a network of understanding generated by what has been done before. In this chapter I would like to focus on what is commonly understood about each genre, and what it therefore means to a writer to balance spontaneity and intention – or freedom and limitation – in the light of that.

Mirroring *vs* Creating

Loosely speaking, we could range the primary genres of writing on a continuum that has "truth to life" at one end (implying that it takes its meaning from reflecting real life), and the self-generation of meaning at the other. Closest to the "truth to life" end would come memoir, then fiction (the novel, short story and novella), and finally poetry, that nimblest of all art forms and probably the most capable of changing our understanding of our experience of the world. In every genre, it's our job as writers to create meaning: that's why it's a continuum. But to varying degrees, all these genres could be said to be expected to reflect "real life", beyond the writing, too.

There are many who would argue – and I among them – that "real life" is a construct, too. Probably the most cogent statement of this point of view for writers is still Samuel Taylor Coleridge's distinction, made in 1817 in the *Biographia Literaria*, between primary and secondary imagination.[47] The first sort of imagination, by which we organise the world we perceive outside of us, and the second, with which we create works of art, differ "only in degree, and in the mode of [their] operation". Like Kant, who argued that we put on notions of time and space like spectacles through which to see the world, Coleridge holds that through primary imagination, we create what we see before us, a "repetition in the finite mind of the eternal act of creation in the infinite I Am". The secondary imagination takes apart that first creation, "dissolves, diffuses, dissipates" it, "in order to re-create", for instance, a work of art.

Glimpses of the oneness that exists prior to that primary act of imagination, such as those that become possible in meditation, or the one I have described experiencing at Cambridge, would certainly seem to support the contention that our agreed-upon subject/object reality, the consensus reality by which we live our practical, daily lives, is a manufactured one. So I'm grateful for Coleridge's reminder that the imagination is everywhere at work, both in what we perceive as external to us, and in the works of art we create. This approach implies that there really can be no such thing as just reflecting, in writing, a reality external to ourselves. In the act of writing, we've already begun to "dissolve" that fixed idea, to perceive meaning in a new way, and to create the world anew. That might be the reason why short-story writer Grace Paley made her famous claim that "any story twice told is fiction".[48] She is not, I hope, saying that any story twice told meets the criteria for a work of fiction; she may well be saying that in the act of writing – or telling – we've already begun to break that external "reality" down, to make choices, to perceive or impute meaning, and to create it anew. By the time we've done that twice, it's playing by its own rules and generating meaning in its own unique way.

Another way to say this is that all writing, insofar as it attempts to create a world for the reader, is metaphoric. Its creations may stand for reality, but they're not continuous with it. It's fundamentally an act of substitution. (When Magritte wrote under his painting of a pipe, "This is not a pipe", he was probably drawing attention to much the same fact about representational art.) And how that act of substitution works, how it has worked before, and how we project that it will work in the future, both generates certain expectations and is limited by them. Those expectations become the evolving conventions of the genre.

Memoir

One of the hardest places for a reader to see how radical an act of substitution is actually taking place is in memoir, conventionally defined as "an account of the personal experiences of an author",[49] "true to the author's memory"[50] and designated as "non-fiction" in every publisher's inventory. Our common expectation of the genre of memoir is that what is written there will be, as far as the writer can tell from her or his own memory, a true account of what actually happened. Lately, freed by the Post-Modern era and its toying with the possibility that language itself may be the primary reality, some successful memoir writers have been challenging the whole notion of a fixed relationship between internal and external truth. "All memoirists lie," says André Aciman,

We alter the truth on paper so as to alter it in fact; we lie about our past and invent surrogate memories the better to make sense of our lives and live the life we know was truly ours. We write about our life, not to see it as it was, but to see it as we wish others might see it, so we may borrow their gaze and begin to see our life through their eyes, not ours.[51]

Granted, there's an air of naughtiness about this statement, as if in saying it, the writer knows he's breaking a taboo. But I believe that what he's fundamentally acknowledging is a truth about writing that all Freefall writers know from observing the first precept: when people drop their pre-conceived intentions for their writing, they make way for the logic of writing itself. Whatever arises then, especially when writers can sense into what has energy for them, will be guided differently, by something deeper, more capacious and altogether wiser than their own rational intentions. Memoirist Patricia Hampl puts it this way:

Perhaps writing is even more profoundly simple, more telegraphic and immediate in its choices than the grating wheels and chugging engine of logic and rational intention suppose. The heart, the guardian of intuition with its secret, often fearful intentions, is the boss. Its commands are what a writer obeys – even without knowing it.[52]

So, in writing a memoir, a writer must be prepared for the fact that whatever his or her lived experience may have been, in the act of writing that experience will be changed. As precisely accurate as we might like it to be, much of what constitutes the memoir will nonetheless emerge *from the act of writing itself,* rather than pop up from some perfect inner record of the past, no matter how evocative and "true to life" it may seem when it's read. "[A writer] does not draw on a reservoir," to quote William Stafford. "Instead, he engages in an activity that brings to him a whole succession of unforeseen stories, poems, essays, plays, laws, philosophies, religions, or –".[53] Or memoirs.

Two Approaches to Memoir

All that said, it seems to me that the strongest convention that exists about memoir is that what is said to be remembered must be "true", if not in the communally agreed-upon, documented sense of history, biography, or autobiography, then subjectively true for the writer nonetheless. Convention also has it that memoir needs to reflect the sense of having been remembered. And, it needs to seem true to the reader when it's read.

Two different approaches in memoir have served all three of these conditions well.

a. The Illusion of the Remembering Mind

In most memoirs, the "enormous degree of blankness, confusion, hunch and uncertainty lurking in the art of writing"[54] that gives birth to the work is concealed in what purports to be the smooth record of some important period in the writer's past, remembered. One of the most frequently-used devices for making that story plausible is what I think of as "the illusion of the remembering mind". This illusion is brought about by the use of an intrusive narrator, who plays out the act of remembering – typically an older, more experienced narrator who looks back at an earlier self. The distance between that older narrator and the younger I-character allows for commentary, irony, dramatic tension and so forth, in the same way it does in fiction. The narrator's memory loops in and out, trolling through whatever territory in the writer's life has been chosen, snagging here and there on a memorable scene, at which point the conditional verbs ("we would go") of the summary give way to the simple past ("that Sunday, we went") and other specifics of a scene. Throughout, the narrator of the memoir is free to comment on, deduce from, marvel at, or hypothesise about whatever is (it is implied) spontaneously being remembered, in a way that keeps that narrator's story (how I got from there to here, for example) present.

Thus in Eudora Welty's *One Writer's Beginnings*, the writer allows the habitual past, such as she offers here, to give way to various specifics:

When we set out in our five-passenger Oakland touring car on our summer trip to Ohio and West Virginia to visit the two families, my mother was the navigator. She sat at the alert all the way at Daddy's side as he drove, correlating the AAA Blue Book and the speedometer, often with the baby on her lap. She'd call out, "All right, Daddy: '86-point-2, crossroads. Jog right, past white church. Gravel ends.' And there's the church!" she'd say, as though we had scored.[55]

But for the most part, her interest lies in combing through that past for news or symbols of her "writer's beginnings" rather than in re-creating the past as such. Hence:

Riding behind my father I could see that the road had him by the shoulders, by the hair under his driving cap. It took my mother to make him stop. I inherited his nervous energy in the way I can't stop writing a story. It makes me understand how Ohio had him around the heart, as West Virginia had my mother. Writers and travelers are mesmerized alike by knowing of their destinations.[56]

Identifying as much with the remembering mind as with the younger person remembered, the reader shares in its back and forth movement between then and now, seeing and deducing, a movement that constitutes much of the drama of the story.

In some memoirs of this type, the reader is invited to see how this very process of remembering has changed the memoirist (as in Nuala O'Faolain's *Are You Somebody?* where the narrator realises that having written the memoir she is now, in fact, somebody). Increasingly, there are memoirs in which the narrator plays with the whole notion of truth in remembering. Lorna Sage's narrator in *Bad Blood*, for example, uses her grandfather's diary (and her grandmother's marginalia) as the jumping-off place for a delightful, refractive series of speculations that leaves us in no doubt about the subjectivity of any one version of remembered experience. Yet at no point in any of these memoirs is the "illusion of the remembering mind" abandoned, nor is the expectation that the material it plays across be "true" (we are never invited to doubt, for instance, that the words Sage offers from her grandfather's diary are the actual words he wrote there). No matter how far the notions of factual truth, the remembering mind, and the conveyed sense of truth are stretched, they still function as fundamental conditions of memoir that continue to be met.

b. The Illusion of Total Recall

An alternative approach to memoir makes very little use of the interventions of the remembering mind, and relies instead on the same illusion that novelists have been relying on since the days of *Robinson Crusoe*: the illusion of total recall. Once the frame or "shell" of an older narrator recalling the past has been established, that older narrator's reality is seldom mentioned again until the end. The past being recalled is re-created more or less seamlessly, and we participate in it much as we would in a novel, seeing virtually everything that transpires there from the younger character's perspective.

Perhaps because the whole notion of total recall requires a leap of faith or credibility, the older narrator often begins by including some reflections on the act of writing or remembering, which serve to keep the sense of memory present. Thus it is in this early passage from Elspeth Huxley's memoir, *The Flame Trees of Thika*:

One cannot describe a smell because there are no words to do so in the English language, apart from those that place it in a very general category, like sweet or pungent. So I cannot characterize this, nor compare it with any other, but it was the smell of travel in those days, in fact the smell of Africa – dry, peppery, yet rich and deep, with an undertone of native body smeared with fat and red ochre and giving out a ripe, partly rancid odour which nauseated some Europeans when they first encountered it, but which I, for one, grew to enjoy.[57]

But such reflections are quickly abandoned, as we move from scene to scene in the life of the child who lived there, with everything "shown" and almost nothing "told" – and with little or no intervention from the remembering narrator:

They rode in silence, and I followed behind them, not at all interested in the conversation, and anxious to get back to Twinkle. Yet I could feel again a tension in the air that made their words memorable.

"There was a scandal when I ran away with Hereward," Lettice said. "You know that I was married before."

"I am afraid all that makes no difference," Ian said, rubbing the backs of his pony's ears with his whip. "But of course it is very interesting."

"Well it is the plot of many hackneyed plays and novels. I was married at eighteen to a man much older than myself [...]"[58]

Here, the "illusion of total recall" has it that this whole conversation actually happened and has been remembered, even by a child who is "not at all interested" in it, and has no idea what's really going on. The slightest excuse (here, "a tension in the air that made their words memorable") is enough to prop up that illusion. These days, not even that much of a nod to the act of remembering seems to be required. But either way, through the convention that total recall is possible, we are plunged deeply into the immediacy of the "remembered" world – so deeply, in fact, that when, inevitably, we return to the older narrator's world at the end of the book, our sense of loss could be said to mirror that narrator's own, the price of having yielded so totally to a past that has now fled.

Writing a Memoir

Coming to memoir from a background in Freefall Writing, you may already have had a good deal of experience in autobiographical writing of the second type. The skills of inhabiting a past self, and of bringing that character's world vividly alive, may be very well-honed. But whether you feel that the essence of your memoir will best be served by the convention of total recall (in other words, by "showing" some segment of the past) or by the convention of an intervening narrator (by "showing" and "telling"), my strong suggestion is that you start by bringing that past to life for yourself first, through Freefall, and then move on to frame it as recall, or bring in the interventions of the remembering mind. In that way, you can truly come to know and identify with the perspective of that past self, and learn what it has to show you, before you go on to consider what the older narrator (you, now) has to say about it.

Writers who try from the outset to write an "intervening narrator" memoir can all too easily find themselves struggling with something that falls fatally between two stools. Repeatedly interrupting their identification with that past self to comment on it, they are often left pondering a past that never truly comes alive on the page. But when they have spent more time with that earlier self and allowed it to flourish as a character, both the vividness of its experience and the wisdom of its perspective will have given the writer both a viable story to work with and something of real substance for that older narrator to comment upon.

As for the content of the memoir, your experience in Freefall may also have made it clear to you what it is you want your memoir to show. As recently as thirty years ago, received wisdom had it that there was no point in trying to write a memoir unless you were famous. The public's pent-up desire to know more about you would in that case already have created a market for your memories. But in the last few decades a thirst has arisen simply to know the details of other people's lives, either on the hoof, in blog form, or recollected in tranquility, as memoir. While "famous person" memoirs have continued to thrive, many people now read memoirs for much more novelistic reasons: to be absorbed in a world they can tell themselves is "real" but that is in some important way markedly different from their own. As crucial as "famous" was to the memoir in the past, so "vivid" and "different" are vital characteristics of many of the memoirs that are eagerly read today.

"Vivid" is a quality you will already have mastered in Freefall, by truly seeing through another character's (often a past self's) eyes, caring about what they care about, and soaking in the sensuous details of their experience. "Different" can come from almost any aspect of the life you have lived, as any memoir-reader knows: an obsession, a particular capacity, or an accident of birth, to name a few. Recently, there has been a noticeable trend for difference to arise from some unique combination: an interest in the inventor of ramen noodles with sex addiction in *The Ramen King and I*, for example, or grieving and reading a novel a day in *Tolstoy and the Purple Chair*; meditation and relationship difficulties in *This Is Not The Story You Think It Is,* or identification with some book or writer as the key to some passage in life (*My Life in Middlemarch*, or *Julie & Julia* for instance).

What role do will and surrender play in all of this? Although both are always alive in any one moment of writing, writing a memoir can call for a sequencing of these two aspects of writing, as well. Surrender will govern that first process, of opening up the area of the past that you want to explore, bringing it alive for yourself and finding out what it has to show you. At that point, intention – what it is you want your memoir to be about – offers you a lens through which to look at that past, whether it's as a commenting narrator, or simply as a writer who is shaping the story of it, discerning what the memoir is going to show, and how. Once you have that lens, then I find it useful to keep this phrase in mind: "it's all about the story." Let everything in your memoir serve that story, such that the choice is not "everything I remember", but "everything I remember about *this*". And remember, should a publisher ask you to put more of a "shell" around an engaging and dramatic story of the past you've written, that will be child's play to accomplish, compared with what you've already done.

Writing Experience

FREEFALL WRITING: CONSCIOUS MEMOIR

Freefall a seminal event in your life – one which you believe has helped to make you what you are today. Apart from the fact that you are approaching this Freefall Writing with intention, observe the five precepts and be sure to allow the scenes to unfold, moment by moment, without commentary. When you've finished, read it over, with a view to seeing what more it can tell you about what has made this event so important in your life.

Now, try going back and inserting a remembering narrator who can act as a guide within the Freefall, commenting upon and thinking about the significance of what you've shown to have occurred. Pay attention to the kind of voice that becomes necessary to make this commentary work.

Writing Tip: Remember that unless you are a famous person whose life is an object of curiosity *per se*, your memoir will be of interest primarily because it is the story of some unique aspect of your life, because it involves the reader, and because the reader can live through it. If you want to create an intervening narrator, create someone who serves and expands the meaning of that story, not someone who wants us to know yet more about who you are, or wants to interpret that story for us.

TIMED EXERCISES: SHOWING WITH TELLING

Write for 15 minutes about one or several of the following topics, preferably taking them to some scene that has meaning for you, and then consider the suggestion that follows:

1. The best days of our lives
2. My fatal flaw
3. Here's trouble!
4. If I had it to do over

5. The mark of Cain
6. Lost time
7. Strong at the broken places
8. How could you forget?

     a. Having written the scene, spend 5 minutes writing about that scene, in any way you think will augment it. Compare how it feels to do that with how it felt to write the scene itself.

     b. Read out both the scene and the commentary to your writing partner, to see if there's anything you're "telling" that you've already "shown".

Writing Tip: Remember to keep "opening out" and "going fearward" with the past you are exploring. The more vividly and candidly your story unfolds, the more easily your readers will be able to slip inside it, and to live these life experiences as their own.

Chapter Eleven
The Genre of Fiction

On the continuum of genres I described in Chapter Ten, with "truth to life" at one end and the self-generation of meaning at the other, the genre of fiction falls in the middle. It is in fiction that these two demands are most evenly balanced. Yes, we want fiction to reflect life as we know it, in some way. Yet we also require that, unlike memoir, it show us a self-consistent world – one that plays by its own rules, and has meaning. No-one comes to a novel, a short story, or a novella expecting to believe, as we do with memoir, that "this really happened". But we do expect that, in one way or another, what we find there will feel true and make sense in relation to itself, in a parallel world of which we might think "this is what happens", or "this could happen", or "this might happen". One of the great satisfactions of reading fiction comes from the fact that the world we find there is to some degree explicable – it answers to its own logic, in ways that the world we live in often does not.

How these two considerations, of truth to life and self-generation of meaning, will play out in each of the main sub-genres of fiction (the novel, short story and novella) is to some extent governed by the conventions of that sub-genre. What those conventions are, how they came about, and what that means for you as a writer coming to fiction from Freefall, is the subject of this chapter.

The Novel

In the earliest days of the novel, some of its chief practitioners took elaborate steps to try to convince their readers that the stories they were reading were factually true. Readers at first believed *Robinson Crusoe*, for instance, to be the actual history of a sailor's experiences, and *Moll Flanders* the memoir of a real felon, because Defoe went to a great deal of trouble to make them appear so. In *Pamela: Or, Virtue Rewarded*, Richardson spends many paragraphs having Pamela, the virtuous maidservant, attest to the truth of her confessions, and she never fails to explain how she came to have writing paper and a pen with her, even when she's hiding in a wardrobe. Non-conformists both, these writers had to contend with the strictures of their faiths about wasting time on sheer entertainment, but that wasn't all there was to it. As memoirists know well, the appeal to factual truth forges an immediate bond with readers, based on their sense of shared humanity, and these early fabulists were not above trying to borrow that effect, however specious, for their own inventions.

But another class of early fiction-writers, whose work was just as vital, had no such inhibitions about entertaining, and apparently no such need to appeal to real life in order to gain effect. Writers from a different social class, they seem to have gloried in fiction's ability to depart from reality at will, with the result that the rollicking improbabilities of *Tom Jones* and the sheer joy in invention in *The Life and Opinions of Tristram Shandy, Gentleman* became just as much a part of the novel's tradition as those other, pseudo-factual undertakings. In fact, these writers openly mocked the idea that what had so obviously been invented could try to masquerade as fact – Sterne through his parodies of memoir-technique in *Tristram Shandy*, and Fielding in his send-up, *Shamela*, where the young maid shows herself to be a liar and a schemer, bartering her virginity for an ever-increasing slice of the estate.

Although, as its name suggests, the novel has never stopped offering its readers other lives they could dream of living, its pretense to being truthful grew more transparent over time, and the formal demands grew stronger. Many of the novel's chief pleasures, like those of drama, came to be found in the ways it could realise what life only hinted at: tensions that could be resolved, problems that found solutions, endings that didn't just stop people dead in their tracks, but provided a satisfactory conclusion. The wandering, episodic plots of the earliest novels made way for more dramatic, wedge-shaped plots (discussed in Chapter Six) that provided an arc of involvement, through an opening development, rising action, climax and denouement.

Increasingly, readers turned to the novel not just to be entertained, or to experience a different life than the one they had chosen, but also to find a world that might shed some light on their own. They came to look to fiction, at least some of the time, not just "to give a faithful report of real-life incidents", to use David Madden's phrase, "but to transform them".[59]

The fact that many novelists write an autobiographical novel at least once in their careers may show that fiction-writers still yearn to appeal to the authority of real life in order to gain legitimacy. But no matter how autobiographical their source material, once writers step inside the genre of fiction, they have to reconcile themselves to its fundamental premise: this is a world where anything and everything can be invented; the suggestion that "this really happened" carries little or no weight at all. Ultimately, a novel stands or falls not on whether it appears to be drawn from life (like a memoir purports to be) but on how life-*like* it feels, and how well it hangs together as a self-contained whole.

Because I work with so many people who come to fiction through Freefall, I often see writers trying to construct a novel that re-shapes their own lived experience, yet contains hints and suggestions that what happens in its pages may be true. These writers run the risk, in my view, of creating work that can't be trusted to be true (it is classified as fiction, after all), yet isn't malleable enough to stand on its own. The weight of what *did* happen in life seems to sink the novel's ability to find its own inner logic. It's as if in wanting readers to marvel at the truth of what really happened, the writer has given up the right to have them marvel at the truth of what can be conceived.

Paradoxically, once your novel has found its own way, whatever autobiographical material does arise can be brought to the service of that inner logic in any way that feels right to you. Novelist John Cheever described this process memorably: "As you dream your ship, you perhaps know the boat, but you're going towards a coast that is quite strange; you're wearing strange clothes, the language being spoken around you is a language you don't understand, but the woman on the left is your wife."[60]

My suggestion is that if, say, certain events in your own life have a draw for you, you freefall them thoroughly. Write your way into every aspect of those experiences, "opening out" whatever seems to you to hold further potential. In this way, you'll be able to bring that past world fully alive for yourself *in writing*, and awaken the suggestive power of whatever transpires in that process. Paradoxically, you'll find that your memory of what actually did happen begins to lose its grip on you, and that whatever constitutes the essence of those events (as discussed in Chapter Three) will begin to emerge in its place: a deeper awareness of what it is that draws you to them, and what for you this particular cluster of events is really about.

Once that transformation has begun to take place, you will begin to feel the sustaining power of your intention. While you remain free to freefall into each scene that comes up for you and to discover what happens there, the project as a whole will be governed by the consideration of how best to bring out its essence, irrespective of what happened in life. Insofar as you have also begun to make the characters your own in that freefalling and opening-out process, you will be able to let them help generate your plot through their conflicts and desires (Chapters Four, Five and Six). You can allow one thing to build on another in the most dramatic way appropriate (Chapter Nine), given the consequences of those characters' choices: the slow working out of free will and destiny in their lives. With virtually everything that happens in the novel as it goes forward, you'll still be able to engage in the kind of surrender in writing that you know so well. None of this needs to be pre-planned unless you want it to be, as long as you keep in the back of your mind the *essence* of what you want it to show.

The length of the novel (typically 80,000 – 400,000 words) has meant that, like a memoir, it has traditionally been comprised of chapters, which create intervals that make the experience of reading something of that length easier to sustain. I sometimes encounter writers who want to write their novels straight through without chapters, a feat that somehow reminds me of Jack Kerouac typing *On The Road* on a roll of paper towel. But chapters offer a novelist unique opportunities that it would be folly to sacrifice. Although a chapter can have as little structure as a "beat" of action does in a play – a "little canter", as one of Beckett's characters calls it – chapters also give the writer the chance to create mini-arcs of story, each with its own rising action, climax, and interim conclusion. They offer a rationale for switching point of view, or plot line. And, perhaps most importantly, chapters have endings: moments of significant power in the narrative that it would be a shame for any novelist to have to do without.

Someone once claimed that there are really only two plots for a novel: "someone takes a trip" and "one day a stranger comes to town". But from the novelist's point of view, it seems to me, both plots are virtually the same. Someone disrupts the status quo, and the rest of the story deals with the outcome of that decision. In that way, the novel is no different from the earliest Greek tragedies, in which the protagonist takes his or her fateful step away from the chorus, and everything else follows from there. But because of the novel's length, that outcome can evolve gradually, through a series of events which open out from one another in whatever ways seem "life-like" to that culture at the time. Unlike a play, the novel is capable of sustaining a complex network of plots and characters, each of which can draw power from the others. And unlike memoir, the novel offers the possibility of using a number of characters' points of view: whatever works best to keep it dramatic while it bears out its fundamental intention.

The Short Story

In the short story, the resemblance to those early Greek dramas – or at least to Aristotle's description of them – is even more striking. Because it is so short (typically less than 5,000 words), it can pounce straight to the heart of the fateful moment of action that characterised those plays. Conventionally, it has also tended to adhere quite closely to the same three "unities" that have long been attributed to Aristotle's discussion of drama:[61] unity of place (a single setting), unity of time (a single day) and unity of action (one particular story line). The moralistic turn of the conclusion of the early short stories (which could be seen as a perversion of *anagnorisis* – insight into the cause of the reversal) has disappeared over time, along with the "mousetrap" or "twist" endings described in Chapter Six. But the short story has never lost its ability to let a single event provoke a striking insight about human life, or to deliver an emotional impact that far exceeds its length.

Over the years, short-story writers have developed their own language for these unities in their genre. One common way of referring to the unity of action is to say that a short story typically contains a moment of which it could be said, "After that, nothing was the same." Another well-known dictum for short-story writers is the question, "Why must it be told today?" (meaning not "Why did you have to tell it today?", but "What is it that makes today the day this action will occur?") – a clear reference to underpinnings of the unity of time. What Alice Adams described as the ABDCE structure of the short story (discussed in Chapter Nine) is also typical of most plays, and one of the most economical ways imaginable to sustain all three unities: begin in the midst of the first action that will lead up to that pivotal moment, provide some background, then let the story proceed steadily to its climax and ending.

The twentieth century saw both a great flourishing in this genre and, often, an ostensible flouting of these conventions. In some of Raymond Carver's stories, where virtually nothing seems to happen, or Alice Munro's sometimes billowing and allusive narratives, it might be difficult to see how those unities are being served. But in fact, given that Carver can depend on his readers' familiarity with the genre, a character's mere expectation that a certain event might happen can be seen as something that could alter the whole course of his life. And one of Munro's great skills is for making an enormous amount of waffling and speculation on the part of a particular narrator suggest its opposite: the existence offstage, as it were, of that one central incident "after which nothing was the same", and which the narrator is at pains to obscure. Like Picasso's mature paintings, these are works by artists who know the conventions of their genre intimately, and just what those conventions will have conditioned their audience to expect.

Freefalling the Short Story

Is a piece of Freefall a short story? If what we mean by that is a story that falls within the genre, and not just a short piece of writing – probably not. Although Freefall writers frequently win short-story competitions with virtually unedited Freefall, I regard many of these events as happy (and very encouraging) accidents, the results of full engagement with a powerful process that brings about a powerful result. But while there is nothing like being unconscious of what you're doing to give the impression of artlessness, the trick is to make it keep happening that way. In the well-known Buddhist parable, if a man stands by a hole in a fence when a rabbit tries to jump through it and hits its head, giving him a dead rabbit for his supper, does the man go back and stand by the same hole a second time?

The shift from what can be achieved naïvely, through full surrender, to what can be brought about with some measure of intention, is a crucial one for Freefall writers to make. The first step is to become aware of what you've spontaneously accomplished that works within this genre, and to file that awareness in the back of your mind, even as you continue to employ the skills of Freefall you've developed so well. Like the first times you tried using the precepts, balancing that surrender with a measure of intention may again feel like learning to ride a bicycle: overbalancing one way, then the other, but finding the position that works almost effortlessly for you in the end. What you write may observe some of the conventions of the short story, or none of them, or it may re-define those conventions altogether, but both what you discover and how you revise will continue to be shaped by what you know.

The Novella

Traditionally, if fiction-writers found that the piece of fiction they were writing promised to be something less complex than a novel but more extended than a short story, they had a third choice: the novella. The popularity of that "little new thing" waned considerably until very recently, because it was so difficult to publish: too long for most magazines, and too short (and too expensive) to publish singly. The few novellas that were published came primarily from well-established writers who had enough of a ready-made following to warrant issuing them in collections (like Stephen King's *Different Seasons*) or singly as a "short novel" (like Ian McEwan's *On Chesil Beach*). But with digital publishing, the novella is now experiencing a resurgence. This is a good

119

thing for fiction writers, because the novella has evolved its own unique conventions over its nearly eight-hundred-year history, which allow writers to say things that otherwise can't be said.

Customarily 20,000 – 60,000 words in length (but for competition purposes, often shorter) a novella can cover an extended drama of unfolding in a way that a short story can't. That slow, fearful journey upriver in Conrad's *The Heart of Darkness*, for instance, could never have been contained by a short story, and yet how could what lay at the end of the journey have achieved its powerful, layered impact in any other way? Unlike most novels, the novella tends to concentrate on a single action (there, the journey upriver to find Kurtz), to make use of a single point of view (in this case, Marlowe's), and – surprisingly often – to be dominated by a single central image or metaphor (there, that of entering the darkness of the human heart). It's hard to imagine the powerful simplicity of a work like *The Heart of Darkness* being altered to meet the more complex demands of the novel. As with every successful work of fiction, it seems to have found the perfect genre for what it had to say.

Freefalling the Novella

Often, Freefall writers ask me whether their lengthy story can be published as a novella – a distinct possibility, in theory, given the number of opportunities online. But given that the question usually seems to come up because a story "just kept growing", I think it's useful to get to know the conventional features of the genre. I find it almost physically helpful to be familiar with the slow, steady progress toward great evil in *The Heart of Darkness*, and the tight, formal structure of *On Chesil Beach*, or *The Picture of Dorian Gray*. Reading these novellas gives me the sense of their weight, which is distinctly heavier than that of a short story, but lighter and less dense than that of a novel. That way, when I perceive the essence of something I'm writing, I seem also to be able to feel into what genre it would be best suited to. There's something in the weight, the heft, that tells me that.

If you do find yourself writing a story that just keeps going, stay open to the insights that arise about its essence. Can enough be left "offstage" for you to convey it as a short story? Does it require the slower pace and cohesive central image of a novella? Or does it seem to be calling for the complex subplots and side-developments of a novel? Whether you choose your genre consciously, or end up in it by default, try to make sure you have a sense of its conventions. That way you can make them work for you, even as you discover what you have to say.

Genre and Meaning

When it comes to considering how writing in any of these genres achieves meaning, I find it's Coleridge, again, who has said it best:

> the common end of all narrative [...] is to convert a series into a whole, to make these events, which, in real or imagined History, move on in a straight line, assume to our understandings a circular motion – the snake with its tail in its mouth.[62]

Something that takes place in time, in other words, is converted in a flash to something that stands outside of time – the *ouroboros* that to the ancient Egyptians symbolised both the beginning of time and the end of it, the snake with a tail in its mouth.

As Coleridge demonstrates in this sentence, those are two different kinds of movement. The flash of understanding we experience when we grasp the essence of a work of fiction, memoir, or poetry is instant and somehow complete, even though in the work in which it expresses itself, events "move in a straight line". A "series" is thus converted "into a whole", and what was a linear movement also becomes a circular one.

For writers, it seems to me, what lies at the heart of that conversion is the action of metaphor, the substitution in which one thing becomes another. In every genre, writing, as I noted at the beginning of the last chapter, acts as a species of metaphor. The creations within those genres may stand for reality, but they're not continuous with it (just as Magritte's painting of a pipe "is not a pipe" in fact). What the writer has achieved is fundamentally an act of substitution, in which two unlike things (the world created within that genre and our understanding of the world outside of it, in this case) become one. It's through enabling readers to make that leap from one to the other that writing becomes able to transform life, rather than simply imitate it. Evolved through

121

repetition, and conditioning expectation, the conventions of the various genres of writing facilitate that leap. *"Let the snake wait under/his weed,"* writes William Carlos Williams,

> *and the writing*
> *be of words, slow and quick, sharp*
> *to strike, quiet to wait,*
> *sleepless*
> *– through metaphor to reconcile*
> *the people and the stones.*[63]

In that "strike" of metaphor in which two disparate things become one, the world we live in flames out with meaning. And that is the work of what Coleridge called our "godlike power", the "secondary imagination": to "reconcile the people and the stones".

Writing Experience

FREEFALL WRITING: THE PIVOTAL MOMENT

Take a piece of autobiographical Freefall that you find memorable. Is there an event in it of which you could say, "After that, nothing was the same?" Or could there be? "Open out" that event into a full scene. Now, freefall two of the events leading up to it, as always showing rather than telling what happens there.

Writing Tip: (another reading tip) Read some classic short stories in which a pivotal moment changes everything: "Runaway" by Alice Munro, "Chef's House" by Raymond Carver, "Everything That Rises Must Converge" by Flannery O'Connor. Now read *On Chesil Beach* by Ian McEwan, and *The End of the Alphabet* by C.S. Richardson, to see how a novella can treat a pivotal moment differently.

TIMED EXERCISES: MEANING AND IMAGE

Write for 15 minutes about several of the following topics, preferably taking them to some scene that has meaning for you, and then consider the suggestions that follow.

1. Was blind, but now I see
2. A leap of faith
3. The last chance
4. A sure thing
5. Believing a lie
6. Between a rock and a hard place
7. A chance encounter
8. Vanished!
9. Not my fault
10. If only

a. Having written the scene, spend 5 minutes writing about what meaning you think that scene has for you. Now, compare how it feels to do that with how it felt to write the scene itself.

b. Now, see if you can come up with one image that could convey that meaning. If you find it helpful, you can begin with the formula, "My/his/her --------- (rage, sense of inferiority, playfulness, joy, jealousy, or whatever it may be) is a -----------" (image).

Writing Tip: Stay curious, both about what you're doing and about what others have done before you. A convention is not a straitjacket, it's just a possibility – and knowledge expands your awareness of what's possible.

Chapter Twelve

Revision

Earlier in this book, I introduced a new precept, "Change anything", with the reminder that "writing is always going to be a voyage of discovery. This fact holds true *even in revision*." Too often, writers are advised at this stage to approach their work from the standpoint of a reader. But revision is part of the creative process, one to which the writer in you still has an enormous amount to offer. The unforeseen insights, breakthroughs and serendipities that have typified all the rest of your writing journey will continue to characterise this phase of the writing as well. Only at the very end of the revision process is it worthwhile, in my view, to imagine yourself as primarily a reader – and perhaps not even then (there are, after all, plenty of real readers out there, all too willing to give their feedback).

Until then, even when you have a full first draft in front of you, the same productive inner balance you have achieved thus far between intention and surrender holds sway. This can be a demanding time for you as a writer. In James Baldwin's words, "You have to strip yourself of all your disguises, some of which you didn't know you had"[64]. Yet for many writers, the revision stage is their favourite. With the safety-net of that first draft beneath you, you can take new chances, risk more, even fall.

What is most helpful, therefore, is to ask yourself the revision questions that will allow your writing self to go further, so that you can take your work to the next level, whatever that may require.

1. Does it need to be revised?

Occasionally, a piece of writing emerges in such a way that it doesn't require any revision. Wordsworth's "Tintern Abbey" is reputed to have come to him whole, and Virginia Woolf, who usually revised obsessively, made virtually no corrections to *To The Lighthouse*. But events like these are exceptional for any writer. As meditation teachers are wont to say of similar experiences of self-transcendence, "The first one comes by Grace. After that, you have to work for it."

But having taken to heart the second precept, "Don't change anything", people who come to writing through Freefall can sometimes experience a particular dilemma at the revision stage. Few skills can be more valuable to a writer than knowing how to achieve the kind of presence on the page that comes from following the precepts, including honouring the way you said something the first time. Fairly quickly in this writing process, the writing emerges looking exceptionally finished and instinctively "right", making it particularly challenging to alter. But now that you've achieved that degree of presence and written your draft, your job is to strip away whatever still veils it, including, wherever necessary, the veil of what you said before.

Accept that whatever you write will almost inevitably need some revising. "Change anything" that seems to you to require changing, trusting that even more acutely evocative words will come to you. Don't allow the safety net of that first draft to become a binding trap.

2. When does it need to be revised?

For many writers, there comes a point while they're writing the first draft, especially of a longer work like a novel or memoir, when the need to go back and revise from the beginning starts to feel like a burning imperative. "I'm using the wrong voice," they say, or "I don't like the way this is going," or "I just haven't done enough research for this to be credible." The only sensible thing at this stage, they feel convinced, is to go back and fix the problem before going on.

Early on, I used to agree with them. If the need to revise had arisen this strongly, surely it had to be acted upon. But I couldn't help noticing how few people who did go back to revise in the middle of their first draft ever went on to finish it. Often, they'd reach the same stage in their draft a second time and the process would repeat itself: "I can't go any further. It's still wrong!"

My conclusion is that this burning urge is yet another "Dragon", like the ones I described in *Writing Without a Parachute* – an internal critical voice, the mistaken purpose of which is to keep the writer safe. The further out on a limb the writer climbs (by continuing to write the draft), the more loudly this voice urges them to go back.

What the voice is telling them may be true. Perhaps there is some problem with the manuscript. But the question the writer needs to ask is, "Why do I have to go back and fix it *now?*" Much better, I think, to bear in mind this trenchant reminder: "If you start to revise before you've reached the end, you're likely to begin dawdling with revisions and putting off the difficult task of writing."[65] Don't try to fix the problem at the level of the problem. You will see everything about your work with different eyes, once you've reached the end.

3. Does fiddling count as revising?

The precepts of Freefall Writing have made it possible for me to write: to trust what occurs to me, to stay on the current of an energy, and even to believe in the way I say things the first time. Nevertheless, I find that every day, when I begin writing, I want to go back and fiddle with what I wrote the day before.

So I do that. I sit and play with the writing for half an hour or so, adjusting a word here, a phrase there, responding to some inner urge to try to make it better. If I look at this activity objectively, it's ridiculous. An utter waste of time. Ultimately I may jettison this entire chapter, and then what will I have gained by all this fiddling?

But still, each day, down in the trenches with the writing, that half-hour of fiddling feels necessary, almost a pre-writing meditation. I like doing it. It pulls me away from the world I've just left, and back into the world of the writing. It also bolsters my ego a little bit, if I'm honest. I find myself thinking, "Look, I wrote this. This is okay". I don't think of this activity as "revision"; certainly, I'm not "re-seeing" anything. I'm playing with words on the page, at least a day away from the time I wrote them. After that, I find I can begin in earnest to write new material.

4. Why does it need to be revised?

To answer this question, you need to return to your sense of the essence of your work – novel, memoir, short story, poem, or whatever the project may be. With that sense of its core purpose clearly in mind, you can ask yourself the question, "Does everything in this writing serve its essence?" If not, you need to revise it. It's that simple. And that fiendishly difficult, too, because to do so really does demand that you become able to view the work from a different perspective. It demands "re-vision".

For one thing, asking yourself that question demands that you penetrate through the surface of the work, moving past what is already in place to ponder what might be there. And that surface can prove to be extraordinarily durable, deflecting you with the scenes or images you've already written or the ways you've written them, especially when you've read and re-read the original version several times already (as I tend to do, while I'm "fiddling"). You can find yourself thinking, "But that's just what happens in this story," whereas the truth is, it doesn't have to be.

Sadly, it may turn out that some of your favourite scenes don't actually serve the story. They may obscure or even detract from its essential thrust. I once heard a suggestion that writers keep a shoebox under their bed, where they can store all their favourite discarded scenes and images, just so they know they still have them. It's an excellent suggestion, if it makes it any easier to let those beloved pages go.

One writer whom I find exemplary in facing the task of "re-seeing" with equanimity is Sandra Gulland, the author of *The Josephine B. Trilogy*, mentioned in Chapter Nine. Gulland reports that when she had finished writing the first novel in the trilogy, she realised that it was simply not the book she had wanted to write. "The novel was in the cracks," is how she puts it. So she set that draft aside and wrote the novel that lay in the cracks. What I find particularly striking is that Gulland claims she went through the same process with all three novels. Each time, she had to write an entire manuscript in order to discover what was waiting to be written. "Now that I know that's how it has to be, I don't really mind it," she says, "It turns out to be just the way I write."

Looking back at your first draft and reading it as the writer, with your sense of its essence in mind, you'll be able to see to what degree your writing fulfills that purpose and what is still "in the cracks" of what you've written.

5. How does it need to be revised?

The answers to this question can depend on what stage you've reached with your manuscript. At the end of the first draft, it's important to ask yourself what can be developed further. Later on, it becomes a question of what can be taken out. It can be useful to leave the work alone for a while (two or three months is good, if you have the time). The characters in scenes you have only just written can exert a strangely magnetic pull on you that weakens over time, releasing you to take up the job of narrator more objectively. While still very much the writer, you may find that at that point you re-engage with the writing in quite a different way.

Once you have completed the first draft and left it alone for a while, some important information about the "how" of this first stage of revision can come from asking the following questions:

a. Does it show what it needs to show?
This question has two parts: first, does it show well enough, and second, does it show enough. To help answer the first one, I often invoke the item from Jack Kerouac's "List of Essentials", mentioned in Chapter Two: "Not to think of words when you stop, but to see picture better". Leave behind what you said before, I take this to mean, and ask yourself, have I seen this scene clearly in my mind's eye? Do I understand the characters well enough? If you've stayed on the surface, you may need to go deeper before you can go on.

I take "picture" not just figuratively but literally, too: do I really see the place where the scene is set? And show that on the page? Especially if a scene takes place in some location you know from life, you can find you've taken too much about it for granted. Only the sensuous details that make their way onto the page will have the power to convey your characters' world instantly, from body to body, as it deserves to be conveyed.

The second part of the question, "Does it show enough?" can certainly mean, "Am I telling what I need to show?" (I once heard a novelist state categorically in an interview that "most of the work a writer needs to do in a second draft is convert 'telling' into 'showing'"). But it can also have to do with daring. "Did I take the jumps?" is another way I ask myself this question. Does the most fraught scene imaginable between these two characters actually take place on the page, or did I side-step it? If the story calls for a moving, climactic speech by one of the schoolchildren (I'm thinking of the film, *Finding Forrester*) did the writer show it, or did they dodge it? (They dodged it.) If an important letter, say, is discovered, did I just describe it, or did I offer a telling excerpt? These are the sort of "jumps" that will take the work to a new level, once you summon the nerve to take them.

b. Is there enough happening?

To answer this question, it helps to imagine filming your characters in any given scene. What are they doing? Are they sitting in a chair (remembering, talking, imagining)? Or are they up on their hind legs, engaged in some action that's significant for the story? I recall Margaret Atwood laughing, in a documentary about her work, at how she had almost reached the end of her first novel when she realised that "nobody had actually done anything yet". And that happens surprisingly often. Yes, vivid things take place in people's minds and in their conversations. But reflection must be balanced by action to make a story come alive.

When you are satisfied that you have supplied all that the first draft of your story had left undone, you will have reached a further stage of revision: the stage of taking out. At this point, a new set of questions arises:

a. Is it compelling?

"Give the reader a reason to turn the page" is how many writers describe the need for their novels (and memoirs) to be compelling. But I prefer Australian writer Peter Temple's more writer-centred version: "I like characters with a reason to get up in the morning."[66] Even if it's not your intention to write a thrilling, tension-packed work of fiction, remember that what compels you (and your characters) has the potential to become compelling on the page. The time has come to ensure that this will happen.

You'll also know from your experience of reading that the sense of being drawn forward is essential. One simple way to enhance this draw is to borrow from the thriller-writers' playbook: "If you want to increase the tension, shorten the time." You'll notice that no matter how clumsily television dramas employ this technique (the murderer who kills on a predictable schedule; the jacket that will blow up in ninety minutes) it always works to compel your attention along.

b. How is the pace?

Another important aspect to consider is whether the story is moving fast enough. In Freefall, the "fearward" precept serves to propel the writer forward. If the hounds of hell are after you, you tend to move fast. In a longer, more purposeful piece of writing – especially if you're enjoying yourself, the inner critic at bay – that kind of momentum can be lost. Remember the dictum I put forward in Chapter Nine: "action advances, description retards." Eliminate what doesn't move the story along – including, if necessary, some of the flourishes in the writing itself. "If it sounds like writing, I rewrite it," claims Elmore Leonard.[67] Draconian, perhaps, but you can use those words to keep you oriented in the right direction.

c. Am I showing too much?

Contrary to what many writers are said to experience about the need to convert 'telling' into 'showing', those who have come into writing through Freefall may find that they need to do the opposite at this stage: to ask, "Are there things I have shown here that I could tell?" What are the most important scenes? Could some of the others be summarised (in the ways discussed in Chapter Nine)? Could two scenes be combined? (The first Timed Writing exercise in Chapter Eight will have shown you one way to do this). Could one scene stand for several that are like it? *You* may have needed to find out what would happen when you wrote a particular scene, but does *the story* need it? This may be the time to synthesise, epitomise, and suggest.

Don't be afraid to allow gaps in your writing, make leaps, and leave things for your reader to explain. I find it enormously helpful to bear in mind this piece of advice: "Always regard your reader as someone just a little more intelligent than you are".[68] A reader has his or her whole mind to think with, whereas as the writer, you will always be limited to whatever you have put down on the page. Once you begin to see your reader as your creative partner, someone who's not just willing but eager to work with you, you'll find there's a lot you can leave to them to accomplish. Don't make the mistake of trying to do everything yourself.

d. Is it time for a "brand new first draft"?

It would be remiss of me not to mention that there is always the possibility, when you have done everything you can conceive of doing to your manuscript, of writing what novelist Jack Hodgins has labelled "a brand new first draft".[69] Indeed, several people recommend it. When you've done everything you can to revise your manuscript, they say, set it aside and write the whole thing over again. Hodgins suggests that this can be a "relaxed and joyful re-telling",[70] "more likely than anything else I can think of to turn up fresh insights, new angles, and original ways of saying things."[71] Anne Lamott describes how, having borrowed against the advance on her second novel, she was forced into a far more desperate version of this undertaking, which eventually met with equally good results.[72]

This kind of radical re-seeing, just when the writer thinks she or he has done enough, has given rise to the sort of tales we hear from publishers: of Alice Munro, for instance, paying for a whole new set of galleys when she realised that a major story, already in proofs, had to be told from a different point of view. Or William Faulkner rewriting one of the first-person stories in *Go Down Moses* from scratch in the third person, and handing the first version to a visiting soldier who later told the tale.

It's not easy, this late in the game, to abandon your hard-won and much-revised manuscript. But the few times a writer I've been working with has rewritten theirs this radically, the results have been spectacular. So allow this question to bubble up in your cauldron of revision prospects: could this work benefit from a "brand new first draft"? You may need courage, or even desperation, but the results can make even this degree of sacrifice worthwhile.

6. What about feedback from readers?

Years ago, I asked Tim Wynne-Jones, novelist and children's writer, what he thought about critiquing groups where writers show their work to several people who read it and make suggestions. His answer was, "They work fine. As long as you take in your eighth draft and tell them it's your first."

I've tested that answer several times over the years and come to the conclusion that he's right: if I show something to a group of readers too soon, the feedback merely confuses me. I need to be far enough along with the work that I can't see any other way to change it. At that point, the story is solid enough that no-one's comments can throw me very far off course. And it's easier to discern, by then, whether or not their suggestions are useful. Worthwhile suggestions usually prompt a sense of recognition, as if they point to something that on some level I must already have known. And those small evasions and manoeuvres that I thought would pass unnoticed? I can rely on a critiquing group to remind me that I can't get away with those, either.

Then, finally, the time has come to let the work go. Off into the world to make a good marriage with the right publisher. Whatever happens now will belong to this new life with its readership. "I thought if I put my work out there, people would come to know me better," one writer complained to me, "but what they're responding to isn't me at all." That's inevitable, given that all writing is "a presence made of absence"[73] which needs whatever the reader will supply. "The tree never eats of its own fruit," is how the ancients put it. Try not to be too attached to the outcome. You've written what you've written. Your job now – and it's a wonderful one – is to move on to your next piece of writing.

Writing Experience

FREEFALL WRITING: FREEFALL REWRITING

Although this is not, strictly speaking, Freefall, it may be timely. Take the worked-over draft of one of your chapters or stories, and make a conscious decision to approach it from another point of view (that of another character) or person (first or third). Now, freefall the whole piece straight through from that new vantage-point (without consulting the existing draft) and see what happens. (Having jumped that hurdle once, you may find it easier to do the same thing another time.)

Writing Tip: Imagine yourself as leaping off one of those four-storey cliffs into the sea. A sense of adventure is your ally, here.

TIMED EXERCISES:

There is nothing like assigning yourself certain tasks you probably need to do anyway, and setting yourself a deadline by which to do them. So try the following:

1. Find an unmet challenge in something you've written: a journal entry one of your characters refers to having written, or the sermon someone is listening to – something you didn't want to try to write yourself. Give yourself 15 minutes to write it, now.

2. Take a pivotal scene you've written in the third person and in 20 minutes, write it in the first.

3. Do the same with a first-person scene, re-writing it in the third.

4. Play around for 10 minutes with an unreliable narrator in the following ways:

a. Think of something your point-of-view character doesn't want to tell someone, and write what they do tell them, instead. When you re-read it, can you infer what they're trying not to say?

b. Faulkner does a wonderful job of conveying what his mentally handicapped character, Benjy, is thinking about in *The Sound and the Fury*, as well as what he's NOT thinking about. Write the thoughts of a character who does not want to think about a traumatic event he or she has just witnessed.

5. Take a scene you've written that feels a bit flat to you and inject some tension into it by shortening the time or increasing the degree of conflict. (It doesn't need to fit into your existing story.) The sky's the limit, so have some fun with this – and try to stay aware of what you do. (20-30 minutes)

Writing Tip: Are you aware of any impulses in the work as it now stands to help people, inform them, or justify yourself? That's what I call a "split agenda". Stay focused on the task at hand, and eliminate whatever doesn't serve the story.

Notes

Chapter One

1. The book was *The I That Is We*, by Richard Moss, M.D. (Berkeley, CA: Celestial Arts, 1981).
2. *Selected Poems of Rainer Maria Rilke: A Translation from the German and Commentary by Robert Bly* (New York: Harper and Row, 1981) 7.

Chapter Two

3. *Evergreen Review* 1:2 (Spring, 1959) 59.

Chapter Four

4. Peter Robb, "Elizabeth Hay explores the power of regret in her new novel", *Ottawa Citizen*, 7 August 2015: D6.
5. *Canadian Writers at Work: Interviews with Geoff Hancock* (Toronto: Oxford University Press, 1987) 212–213.
6. *Aristotle's* Poetics: *Translated and with a Commentary by George Whalley*, ed. John Baxter and Patrick Atherton (Montreal and Kingston: McGill-Queen's University Press, 1997) 85–87.

Chapter Five

7. *Aspects of the Novel*, ed. Oliver Stallybrass (London: Penguin Books, 2000, 1927) 57.

8. *Laughter: An Essay on the Meaning of the Comic* 1:1, trans. Cloudesley Brereton and Fred Rothwell <http://www.gutenberg.org/files/4352/4352-h/4352-h.htm> first posted January 14, 2002; posting date: July 26, 2009.

9. *The Intimate Merton*, ed. Patrick Hart and Jonathan Montaldo (San Francisco: HarperCollins, 1999) 10.

10. Ibid.

Chapter Six

11. Private correspondence, January 11, 1996.

12. *The Writer's Chapbook: A Compendium of Fact, Opinion, Wit, and Advice from the 20th Century's Preeminent Writers*, ed. George Plimpton (New York: Viking, 1989) 191–192.

13. Ibid, 188.

14. Ibid, 187.

15. Ibid, 191.

16. Ibid, 190.

17. *Writing Fiction: A Guide to Narrative Craft* (New York: HarperCollins, 1992) 40.

18. Laura Miller. "Making a Monster." *Salon* July 1, 1999 < http://www.salon.com/1999/07/01/oleander>

19. "At the time I begin writing a novel, the last thing I want to do is follow a plot outline. To know too much at the start takes the pleasure out of discovering what the book is about." Elmore Leonard. "Making It Up as I Go Along" *AARP Magazine* July & August 2009 < http://www.elmoreleonard.com/index.php?/weblog/more/making_it_up_as_i_go_along_-_elmores_aarp_essay_online>

20. *Aristotle's* Poetics, 87.

21. Ibid.

22. *Selected Tales of Guy De Maupassant*, ed. Saxe Commins (New York: Random House, 1945) 144.

23. *The Collected Works of C. G. Jung,* trans. R.F.C. Hull (London: Routledge, 1977) 9ii para 126.

Chapter Seven

24. John Gardner, *The Art of Fiction: Notes on Craft for Young Writers* (New York: Random House, 1991,1984) 97.
25. (New York: Riverhead Books, 2001) 64-65.
26. (Toronto: Alfred A. Knopf Canada, 2011), 149.
27. *The Big House* (London: Bloomsbury, 2000) 2.
28. (New York: Berkley Publishing Group, 1999) 55.
29. (London: Penguin Books, 2007, 1958) 214-215.
30. *A Writer's Diary: Being Extracts from the Diary of Virginia Woolf,* ed. Leonard Woolf (London: The Hogarth Press, 1953) 139.
31. In a notebook entitled "Notes for Writing", Woolf wrote under the heading,"To the Lighthouse", "two blocks joined by a corridor". "Articles, Essays, Fiction and Reviews 1924-1940" Holograph Notebooks, Vol. 2. Henry W. and Albert A. Berg Collection, the New York Public Library. New York.
32. Raymond Carver, *Cathedral* (New York: Random House, 1984, 1981) 62.

Chapter Eight

33. David Madden, *Revising Fiction: A Handbook for Writers* (New York: Barnes & Noble Books, 2002, 1988) 154.
34. Harold Pinter, *The Caretaker and The Dumb Waiter* (New York: Grove Press, 1988, 1960) 11.
35. *A Passion for Narrative: A Guide for Writing Fiction* (Toronto: M&S, 1993) 113.
36. "Writers on Writing; Easy on the Adverbs, Exclamation Points and Especially Hooptedoodle", *The New York Times,* July 16, 2001.
37. *A Backward Glance* (New York: D. Appleton-Century Company, 1934) 203.

Chapter Nine

38. Auberon Waugh, on the cover of *Harriet Said* (London: Fontana Paperbacks, 1982, 1972).

39. *Harriet Said*, 7.

40. Ibid, 9.

41. This acronym is attributed to short-story writer Alice Adams by Anne Lamott, in *Bird By Bird: Some Instructions on Writing and Life* (New York: Doubleday, 1994) 62.

42. *A Passion for Narrative*, 162-163.

43. David Madden calls putting descriptive details "in a lump" at the beginning of a piece of writing,"the setting fallacy" (*Revising Fiction*, 175).

44. *Night Travellers* (Winnipeg: Turnstone Press, 1982) 60.

45. An interesting example is Sarah Ferguson's memoir, *A Guard Within* (London: Chatto & Windus, 1973).

46. "Writers on Writing; Easy on the Adverbs, Exclamation Points and Especially Hooptedoodle", *The New York Times,* July 16, 2001.

Chapter Ten

47. Samuel Taylor Coleridge, *Biographia Literaria* Chapter XIII *Project Gutenberg*. Web. 26 January 2013. <http://www.gutenberg.org/files/6081/6081-h/6081-h.htm> All ensuing quotes are from this explanation.

48. Quoted in Nancy Adams, *The Other Mother* (Madison: University of Wisconsin Press, 1999) xi.

49. "Memoir" *American Heritage Dictionary of the English Language,* 5th ed. 2011. Houghton Mifflin Harcourt Publishing Company. Web. 21 Mar. 2016. <http://www.thefreedictionary.com/memoir>

50. "Memoir" John F. Kilstrom, UC Berkeley. Web.14 September 2015. <http://socrates.berkeley.edu/~kihlstrm/memoir.htm>

51. "A Literary Pilgrim Progresses to the Past", *Writers [on Writing]* (New York: Times Books, 2001) 6.

52. *I Could Tell You Stories* (New York: W.W. Norton & Company, 2000) 28.

53. *Writing the Australian Crawl* (Ann Arbor: The University of Michigan Press, 1978) 17.

54. Hampl, 27.

55. (New York: Warner Books, 1985, 1984) 47.

56. Ibid, 48.

57. (Harmondsworth: Penguin Books, 1962, 1959) 10.

58. Ibid, 126.

Chapter Eleven

59. *Revising Fiction*, 8.

60. Quoted by Sue Miller in "Virtual Reality: The Perils of Seeking a Novelist's Facts in her Fiction", *Writers [On Writing]*, 156.

61. Only the unity of action is described at any length in the *Poetics*, with a brief mention given to the unity of place. However, the recommendation that playwrights observe all three unities has been ascribed to him since the seventeenth century.

62. From an undated letter in Joseph Cottle, *Reminiscences of Samuel Taylor Coleridge and Robert Southey* (London: Houlston and Stoneman, 1848) 347.

63. "A Sort of a Song", *The Collected Poems of William Carlos Williams: Volume II. 1939–1962* (New York: New Directions Books, 1988, 1946) 55.

Chapter Twelve

64. *The Writer's Chapbook*, 126.

65. Pearl S. Buck, excerpted from *Writer's Yearbook, 1963* in "How I Write", *Writer's Digest* December 1995, 29.

66. "The Unvarnished Truth", *The Weekend Australian*, October 3–4, 2009.

67. "Writers on Writing; Easy on the Adverbs, Exclamation Points and Especially Hooptedoodle", *The New York Times,* July 16, 2001.

68. A suggestion made by poet Dale Zeiroth.

69. *A Passion for Narrative*, 237.

70. Ibid.

71, Ibid.

72. *Bird By Bird*, 86–92.

73. Jacques Lacan, *Écrits: A Selection*, trans. Alan Sheridan (London: Tavistock Publications, 1977) 65.